Look, Learn & Create

Crochet

A WORKSHOP
101
IN A BOOK

QUARRY

Brimming with creative inspiration, how-to projects, and useful information to enrich your everyday life, Quarto Knows is a favorite destination for those pursuing their interests and passions. Visit our site and dig deeper with our books into your area of interest: Quarto Creates, Quarto Cooks, Quarto Homes, Quarto Lives, Quarto Drives, Quarto Explores, Quarto Gifts, or Quarto Kids

© 2012 Quarto Publishing Group USA Inc.

This paperback edition published in 2018

First Published in 2012 by Creative Publishing international, an imprint of
The Quarto Group, 100 Cummings Center, Suite 265-D, Beverly, MA 01915, USA.
T (978) 282-9590 F (978) 283-2742
QuartoKnows.com

Quarry Books titles are also available at discount for retail, wholesale, promotional, and bulk purchase. For details, contact the Special Sales Manager by email at specialsales@quarto.com or by mail at The Quarto Group, Attn: Special Sales Manager, 401 Second Avenue North, Suite 310, Minneapolis, MN 55401, USA.

10 9 8 7 6 5 4 3 2 1

ISBN: 978-1-63159-652-0

Digital edition published in 2018
eISBN: 978-1-61058-419-7

Originally found under the following Library of Congress Cataloging-in-Publication Data
Burger, Deborah.
Crochet 101 : master basic skills and techniques easily through step-by-step instruction / Deborah Burger.
p. cm.
Summary: "Beginner's guide to crochet, teaching all the basic techniques through easy projects." Provided by publisher."
ISBN 978-1-58923-639-4 (spiral bound)
1. Crocheting. I. Title.
TT820.B95 2012
746.43'4--dc23
    2012010571

Technical Editor: Karen J. Hay
Stitch Illustrations: Karen Manthey
Proofreader: Julie Grady
Cover & Book Design: Mighty Media, Inc.
Page Layout: Danielle Smith
Step-out Photographs: Eleanor Dotson Carlisle
Videographer: Henry Felt

Printed in China

CONTENTS

Introduction

Welcome to the versatile, creative world of crochet! Crochet 101 *is designed to help you learn painlessly, building each new skill on the success of those you've mastered, and to grow your confidence as each chapter enables you to create a beautiful and useful project. Easy-to-follow instructions with lots of colorful photographs help you gain crochet skills step-by-step. Along the way, you'll create accessories, toys, garments, and home décor items with great appeal!*

A versatile fiber art, crochet can create softly draping fabric for shawls and sweaters, firm 3-dimensional stuffed toys and sculptures, sturdy or delicate fabrics according to need. With its limitless possibilities in form and function, crochet is enjoyed by millions of people of all ages and genders, worldwide. The universal stitch symbols you'll learn in this book mean that patterns are shared across usual boundaries of language and culture, opening wide the doors to creative expression.

Each chapter of *Crochet 101* introduces a new stitch or technique. You'll practice that skill, and then use it in making a beautiful project. The new skill or skills in each chapter are listed in the section labeled **What You'll Learn.** Supplies and materials for the lesson and its project are listed as **What You'll Need. Troubleshooting** boxes will help you evaluate the quality, possible mistakes, and means of correcting them, in your work as you progress. **Quick Reference** and **Crochet Language** boxes explain terms and processes without requiring you to turn to another page. **Tips** offer the sort of specific encouragement that builds confidence and ensures mastery. Each project specifies a particular yarn, but also includes suggestions for substitution. Projects can be made in the colors shown, or in your own favorites, and many projects also include suggestions for optional variations—ways to further personalize your crochet.

The first section, Chapters 1-6 "Crochet Basics," acquaints you with the tools, materials, and methods for making basic crochet stitches in rows and in the round. When these chapters and projects are completed, you'll have achieved an "Advanced Beginner" skill level, and will find a world of possibilities open to you. The second section, Chapters 7-12 "Putting It All Together," moves beyond the basics into the realm of textured and shaped fabric, pattern-stitches, and more complex sets of directions. The projects in this section include textural fabrics forming fitted accessories and garments. The final section, Chapters 13-16 "Crochet Traditions," introduces some of the traditional styles of crochet: Thread Lace, Filet Crochet, and Tunisian Crochet; and offers tips and tricks to add excellence to finished projects and make construction easier. When the last project is completed, you'll be a solid and confident Intermediate Crocheter, ready to independently learn any advanced or specialized technique that appeals to you. You'll be able to read and follow standard patterns and diagrams, or crochet creatively from your own ideas.

Start each chapter by reading through the **What You'll Learn** and **What You'll Need** boxes. Make sure the tools and materials for the lesson are at hand, so your learning and practice are not interrupted. Follow the written instructions and photographs, and don't skip the

INSTRUCTIONS
Note: Stitch counts appear in {brackets} following instructions for the round.

Foundation: Ch 4, sl st to join in a ring.

Crown of Hat
Rnd 1: Ch 1, work 6 sc in ring. PM in first st made, and in each following rnd, MM to keep it always in first st of rnd. Do not join, work progresses in spiral. {6 sc}

Rnd 2: 2sc in each st around. {12 sc}

Rnd 3: *2 sc in next st, sc in next st; repeat from * around. {18 sc}

Rnd 4: *2 sc in next st, sc in each of next 2 sts; repeat from * around. {24 sc}

Rnd 5: *2 sc in next st, sc in each of next 3 sts; repeat from * around. {30 sc}

Rnd 6: *2 sc in next st, sc in each of next 4 sts; repeat from * around. {36 sc} Check gauge before proceeding.

Rnd 7: *2 sc in next st, sc in each of next 5 sts; repeat from * around. {42 sc}

Rnd 8: *2 sc in next st, sc in each of next 6 sts; repeat from * around. {48 sc}

Rnd 9: *2sc in next st, sc in each of next 7 sts; repeat from * around. {54 sc}

Checking gauge on Rnds 1–6.

Rnd 10: *2 sc in next st, sc in each of next ... repeat from * around. {60 sc}

Rnd 11: Sc in each st around. {60 sc}

Rnd 12: 2sc in next st, sc in each of ... repeat from * around. {66 sc}

TIP The increase pattern changes ... Rnd 10, to begin cupping the ... of the hat.

Troubleshooting
Counting rounds. When sc is worked in spiral rounds, each round appears as a ridge, ... Starting at the center of the piece, where the first ring is Rnd 1, count the ridges strai... stitch to the right of the marked stitch. This count will tell you how many rounds are ... moment. To keep track of rounds in the written pattern, many crocheters use a sma... it from row to row through the pattern's text.

46   Crochet 101

WHAT YOU'LL LEARN
- How to make WS (wrong side) dc clusters in alternating rows of a fabric
- How to make puff or "raspberry" stitches in either side of a fabric
- How to use tall (tr) stitches between short stitches to create WS mini-bobbles

WHAT YOU'LL NEED
YARN
- Smooth textured, solid-colored, worsted-weight yarn

HOOKS
- Size H (5 mm) or I (5.5 mm)

these patterns are worked on the wrong side rows of a fabric, pushing the textured stitch to the right side. Therefore, the right side rows of the fabric are worked in plain row of sc or dc stitches. These stitch patterns show up best when a smooth textured yarn is used—one without much "fuzz" or halo. It's also best to use a plain or monochrome colored yarn, rather than a variegated one, to enhance the appearance of textured stitches. Too much variety in both surface and color tends to confuse the eye, and make it difficult to appreciate the textured stitching.

Let's start with Cluster Bobbles, since the process of decreasing by working two stitches together is already familiar.

HOW TO MAKE 3-DC CLUSTER BOBBLES
The RS (right side) rows of the fabric can be any stitch—sc or dc are most commonly used. These non-textured rows form what's called the "background fabric" from which the bobbles stand out in relief. Our swatch will start with a background fabric of sc. After a few rows, we'll switch to a dc background, so the difference in drape and softness of the fabric is evident. Each type of background is appropriate for different sorts of projects, depending on function and appearance.

QUICK REFERENCE
Clusters or Cluster Stitches consist of a number of stitches begun and each worked to their last loop. The final yarn over and pull through unites all the stitches in one at the top. Clusters differ from decreases in that a decrease has the partial stitches made by inserting the hook into successive stitches, while a cluster's stitches all begin in the same stitch or space. Some older patterns denote a decrease by saying, "work a 2dc cluster over next 2 sts." This lets the crocheter know that the partial stitches will be spread over the space of 2 stitches in the preceding row, but will "finish" together as one stitch, reducing the number of stitches in the row by one. A regular cluster does not change the stitch count, as it begins in one stitch or space, and is completed as a single stitch in the new row. When the stitches comprising the cluster are taller than the adjacent stitches in their row, they bend outward toward the opposite side of the fabric, creating a bobble. Clusters may contain any number of partial stitches, and a well-written pattern will define its particular cluster in the "Stitches Used" section.

Symbol diagram for 3-DC cluster bobbles.

1 Start with a chain of 29 (multiple of 8 + 5).

Row 1 (RS): Sc in 2nd ch from hook and each ch across {28 sc}

Row 2 (WS): Ch 1, sc in each of first 2 sts, in next st work (yo, insert hook and draw up a loop, yo and pull through 2 loops) 3 times.

(continued)

Putting It All Together   115

"Practice Swatches." Practice pieces are not a waste of time; they add to your understanding of the skill, and train your hands in their new task, before beginning the project. Even Advanced and Expert crocheters begin new projects with practice swatches, so it's a very good habit to start. Use the **Troubleshooting** boxes and **Tips** to evaluate and improve your stitching, and then you'll be ready for the chapter's project.

The video tutorials created to supplement this book are an additional learning tool demonstrating the essential techniques used in crochet. You can access the video at this web site: **www.qbookshop.com/pages/crochet101**.

Most of all, have fun with these crochet projects. Enjoy your own blossoming creativity as you learn new skills.

Crochet Basics

There's no better place to start than at the very beginning. In writing this book, we assume you're starting from scratch, and we know that for a new crocheter, even a trip to the yarn shop or crafts store can be challenging. There is an almost overwhelming variety of pattern leaflets, yarns, crochet hooks, and notions to choose from. To give you a firm foundation for learning to crochet, this section starts with essential facts about hooks and yarns. Next, you'll learn the basic stitches and the written language of crochet patterns. If crochet is completely new to you, you'll appreciate the detailed information and photos. Even if you have some crochet experience, you'll probably learn something new.

It's important to remember that you're training the muscles of your hands and fingers in movements new to them. Be patient with yourself—muscle memory develops by repetition. The process of learning will be more enjoyable if you give yourself permission to be a beginner. Mistakes are a normal and natural part of the process. Holding and moving the hook and yarn will seem awkward at first; that's also part of the process. Relax! Stretch your shoulders and hands often; don't forget to breathe. Speed is not a measure of success, so feel free to stitch slowly, to take frequent breaks, and to enjoy the feeling of yarn passing through your fingers.

Let's explore the basics of crochet!

CHAPTER 1: Getting Started

The Tools

At its simplest, crochet can be done with no tools at all, using the fingers to pull loops of yarn through other loops. But over the years, crocheters have found that a specialized hook eases the work and makes it possible to create much more complex and beautiful stitches. Generally, the only current uses for "finger crochet" are keeping lengths of electrical cord from tangling and keeping children occupied when they must sit still. All "real" crochet involves a hook of one sort or another, so let's take a look at the crochet hook.

THE CROCHET HOOK

Hooks come in several different sizes and shapes, depending on their intended uses. But they all have the same parts, labeled in the photo below.

The tip of the hook is the part that's inserted between strands of yarn, and tips vary in shape from blunt to more pointed. The throat (or shank) and chin of the hook are the parts that do the actual work, catching a loop of yarn and pulling it through other loops. The shaft is what gives the hook its official size, and the size of the shaft determines the size of the loops made. Some hooks have a thumb rest and some don't. When present, the thumb rest can make it easier to hold the hook, and also to loosen loops that have become too tight. On some brands of hooks, the thumb rest has been expanded into an ergonomic handle— crocheters with arthritis, carpal tunnel syndrome, and other hand health issues find that these handles help to keep their crochet hobby possible and pain-free. Some hooks, especially those made of wood, have decorative turning or carving at the end of the shaft. This shaping can help to provide balance, but is mostly an aesthetic element.

There are two basic shapes for hooks, and most crocheters find that they prefer one or the other. It's a good idea to try some crochet with each shape in the first few projects to discover which shape is the best for your own hands. Many crocheters find it extremely frustrating and difficult to work with the "wrong" hook shape, and **only** experimentation can determine the "right" hook for any particular crocheter. The major difference between the two kinds of hooks is in the shape of the throat.

An "inline" hook, also called a "Bates-shape" hook, has a throat as wide as the shaft, and the chin is formed by a straight cut into the hook's throat. Inline hooks usually have relatively blunt tips.

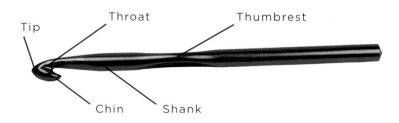

Tip · Throat · Thumbrest · Chin · Shank

Left to right in each pair:
Boye/tapered hook, Bates/inline hook.

The second major hook shape is the tapered or "Boye-shape" hook. Its throat becomes narrower from side to side as it approaches the tip, and the cut under the chin is also tapered. Tapered hooks usually have a relatively more pointed head. These names for the major hook shapes reference the two major companies that have provided crochet hooks for the last century, but many other companies and individuals now also create crochet hooks, using these standard shapes.

The hooks shown in use throughout this book are tapered, or Boye-shape hooks, but that by no means implies superiority—it's simply the shape that works best for the author.

Hooks are available in a wide variety of materials as well as a wide variety of sizes. Tiny steel hooks are generally used for crocheting lace from cotton or silk thread. They are made of steel because threadwork requires tight tension and hooks made of other materials and small enough for threadwork can bend, or even break, in use. Steel hooks are also appropriate for crocheting with wire in making jewelry. Steel hooks have their own sizing/naming system, different from the system used for all other hooks. Commonly available steel hook sizes start with 00, the largest, and progress through 14, with higher numbers denoting smaller hooks. This is similar to the system of "gauge" for steel wire.

The other most common materials for hooks are aluminum, wood, and bamboo. These larger hooks are usually used for crochet with yarn and other fibers. Whether made from these or other materials, such as glass or stainless steel, these hooks are commonly sized in the United States by a letter system. The system is not perfect, and leaves gaps—sizes with no name. It's gradually being replaced by simple measurements in millimeters. Many hooks are labeled with both a letter and a measurement, but letters alone are also still quite common. Generally .25 mm or .50 mm is the difference between two sizes, and the sizes with assigned letters are the easiest to find in craft stores.

Some older hooks and some custom made hooks are not labeled with their sizes, and sometimes the labels wear off with time and use. An inexpensive gauge tool, which will be discussed later, solves the "mystery hook" problem

TIP While working through the first few chapters, try out both shapes of hook, and then decide which works best for you!

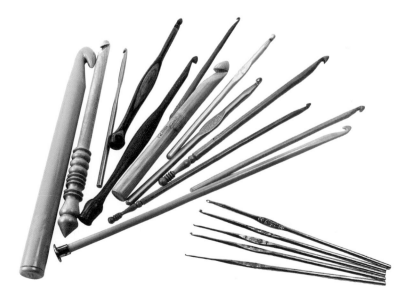

Steel Hook Sizes

00	=	2.70 mm
0	=	2.55 mm
1	=	2.35 mm
2	=	2.20 mm
3	=	2.10 mm
4	=	1.75 mm
5	=	1.70 mm
6	=	1.60 mm
7	=	1.50 mm
8	=	1.40 mm
9	=	1.25 mm
10	=	1.15 mm
11	=	1.05 mm
12	=	1.00 mm
13	=	0.95 mm
14	=	0.90 mm

Aluminum Crochet Hook Sizes

B/1	=	2.25 mm
C/2	=	2.75 mm
D/3	=	3.25 mm
E/4	=	3.5 mm
F/5	=	3.75 mm
G/6	=	4 mm
7	=	4.5 mm
H/8	=	5 mm
I/9	=	5.5 mm
J/10	=	6 mm
K/10½	=	6.5 mm
L/11	=	8 mm
M/N/13	=	9 mm
N/P/15	=	10 mm
P/Q	=	15 mm
Q	=	16 mm
S	=	19 mm

Sizes are commonly labeled on thumbrest or shaft.

FIBERS FOR CROCHET

Crochet consists of looped fiber. We've discussed the hook that creates the loop, but it's also important to understand some of the variety of materials that wrap around the hooks! Besides the traditional white cotton or silk thread, crocheters commonly use yarn made of various fibers, which is available in a variety of sizes. The size or thickness of the yarn is as important as the size of the hook, to determine the softness or firmness, drape or stiffness, of the fabric created; each type and size of yarn has appropriate uses. The packaging of yarn or thread usually gives information about the thickness, fiber content and its care, and length in yards or meters, of the hank or ball. We'll examine those labels closely later, but let's look at the types of fiber first.

Thread

Many of the traditional uses of crochet involved making lace from thread. Most thread made for crochet is cotton. It's available in both "mercerized" and unmercerized states. Thread consists of very tightly spun fibers, and has no ability to stretch when pulled. Any stretch in the fabric is produced by the particular stitches used, and still has very little "memory" or ability to bounce back to its original shape after being stretched. Mercerization is a finishing technique in the spinning process, and is used to give a high polish to the thread. Mercerized cotton has a slight sheen to its surface; it also glides more easily into loops and over the hook. This attribute can either be wonderful . . . or a problem, for a particular project, and the designer of a lace pattern will usually specify whether it's intended for mercerized cotton or not. Mercerization reduces the cotton's ability to absorb moisture, but adds beauty to the finished object. A tablecloth, for instance, might be made of mercerized cotton to reduce absorption of stains and spills and provide a polished appearance. On the other hand, unmercerized thread creates lace for garments that is less stiff and scratchy feeling, because it

has less polish on its surface. Thread is available in numbered sizes, and like the steel hooks, the higher numbers denote finer threads. "Bedspread Cotton" or #10 thread is the most common size. #5 cotton thread is commonly used for summer garments and accessories, as is #3, "Perle Cotton." Embroidery floss is another form of cotton thread sometimes used for crochet. Its brilliant colors can provide wonderful accents in white or ecru lace. Perle Cotton and embroidery floss are usually sold in twisted or folded hanks, which must be wound into balls before use for crochet, or terrible tangling will result. Thread in size 5 and 10 are usually wound on a cardboard spool or cone, ready for immediate use. The finest threads, sizes 30-80, are not as commonly available, and are used for the most delicate laces.

Yarn

The word "yarn" refers to fibers spun much more loosely than thread. Yarn, even when actually thinner than thread, is distinct because the looser spin allows it to stretch. Crocheting with yarn requires less tension in the hands, and provides a wide variety of finished effects. Regardless of the fiber content, yarn is categorized by size. The Craft Yarn Council of America has developed a set of standard size ranges, and project patterns refer to these names and numbers.

STANDARD YARN WEIGHT SYSTEM
Categories of yarn, gauge ranges, and recommended needle and hook sizes

Yarn Weight Symbol & Category Names	0	1	2	3	4	5	6
Type of Yarns in Category	Fingering 10-count crochet thread	Sock, Fingering, Baby	Sport, Baby	DK, Light Worsted	Worsted, Afghan, Aran	Chunky, Craft, Rug	Bulky, Roving
Crochet Gauge* Ranges in Single Crochet to 4 inch	32–42 double crochets**	21–32 sts	16–20 sts	12–17 sts	11–14 sts	8–11 sts	5–9 sts
Recommended Hook in Metric Size Range	Steel*** 1.6-1.4 mm	2.25—3.5 mm	3.5—4.5 mm	4.5—5.5 mm	5.5—6.5 mm	6.5—9 mm	9 mm and larger
Recommended Hook U.S. Size Range	Steel*** 6, 7, 8 Regular hook B-1	B-1 to E-4	E-4 to 7	7 to I-9	I-9 to K-10½	K-10½ to M-13	M-13 and larger

* GUIDELINES ONLY: The above reflect the most commonly used gauges and needle or hook sizes for specific yarn categories.

** Lace weight yarns are usually knitted or crocheted on larger needles and hooks to create lacy, openwork patterns. Accordingly, a gauge range is difficult to determine. Always follow the gauge stated in your pattern.

*** Steel crochet hooks are sized differently from regular hooks—the higher the number, the smaller the hook, which is the reverse of regular hook sizing.

Craft Yarn Council of America

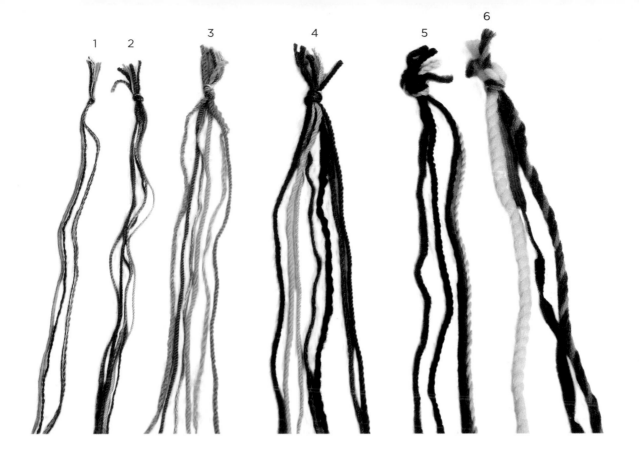

You'll notice that each of the categories is actually a range of sizes, and while all yarns labeled with that number fall within its range, there can still be some variety between the size of different yarns within the same category! A thin "worsted" (#4) yarn might be nearly identical to a yarn at the thick end of the "light worsted/ DK" (#3) category. The system is a guide when choosing yarns, but it's important to remember that not all yarns in one category will necessarily make good substitutes for one another.

Besides size differences, yarn is made from many different materials. Cotton yarn is similar in some ways to cotton thread, except that it's spun more loosely. Worsted (#4) cotton yarn is often called "kitchen cotton" and is used for making highly absorbent and often beautiful dishcloths and towels. However, cotton yarn can also be used to make sweaters, scarves, and other accessories, especially when blended with other fibers. Cotton's ability to absorb moisture makes it a great choice for summer garments. Wool is spun from sheeps' fleece, and has several wonderful properties. It is the only fiber that can help retain body heat even when wet. Wool also repels water, and has great stretch memory. Other animals' hair is also commonly spun into yarn, as well: alpaca is the warmest fiber, but has a very delicate structure; mohair is sturdy and can add a fuzzy or "haloed" texture to yarn, and to the fabric made from it; llamas, yaks, camels, and angora rabbits also provide very soft hair for yarn.

TIP Yarn purchased in loose skein form needs to be wound into balls before use. Many yarn shops will wind balls if asked, or the skein can be draped over the back of a chair and wound by hand. Never attempt to crochet directly from a hank or looped skein, as it will result in terrible tangles!

Yarn Vocabulary

Smooth or plain—just as it sounds, no real discernable texture to the yarn. Plain textured yarns are the easiest to crochet with, and allow special textures in the actual stitches to show to best advantage.

Loft—the ability of a yarn to be squeezed smaller (feel "squishy"), and to naturally expand to fill space. Loft is created by air space between the fibers in the yarn.

Twist—the tightness and direction that the fibers are spun together to create the yarn.

Ply—smaller strands of spun fiber that are twisted together to create yarn. A "single" is not plied; its fibers are spun in only one direction. When singles are twisted together, they form a yarn less likely to kink and knot in use. "Worsted" yarn is often made of 4 plies; DK or "Sport" of 3.

Halo—any visible fibers sticking out from the main, twisted core of the yarn. These create a fuzzy texture in the yarn, and in fabric made from the yarn.

Thick and thin—just as it sounds. Some yarns are intentionally varying in their diameter. These yarns are then sized by averaging the thickest parts and thinnest parts, to fit in the CYCA sizing system.

Slubs—as the word sounds, slubs are intentional blobs of unspun or knotted fiber, included in the yarn to add textural interest.

Bouclé—refers to loops in yarn, created by twisting two plies together at different rates of speed. The loops can be large or small, and create a haloed effect, as the loops spread out from the yarn's core.

Bloom—refers to a yarn's ability to expand or develop a halo after the fabric is made. Yarns that bloom may start out with a smooth or plain texture, but later develop a fuzzy surface. The hair of angora rabbits is often included in luxury yarns, and will work its way to the surface and bloom once the project is complete. This characteristic can make it easier to create fuzzy surfaces, since the yarn "works" like a plain yarn, and develops its softer surface later. However, yarns that bloom are not a good choice for showing off textured stitching.

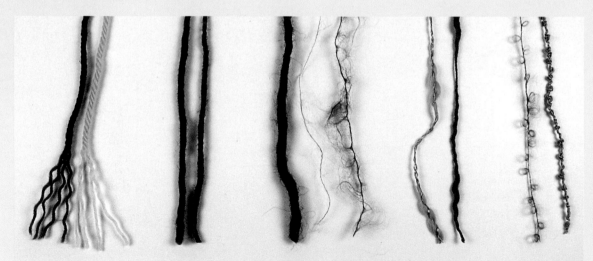

From left to right: smooth or plain with several plies, smooth single, yarns with halo, plied thick and thin with slubs, bouclé yarn

NOTIONS

Besides a hook and yarn, there are many notions to choose from. Only a few of them are essential, though! The necessary notions are:

Scissors—a small, pointed pair of sharp scissors will make it easy to be accurate in cutting yarn exactly where it needs to be cut.

Large-eyed yarn needle—used for weaving tails of yarn into the completed fabric, and for sewing together pieces of a project. Needles are available in either plastic or steel, but steel tends to glide through the fabric more easily, enhancing the accuracy and invisibility of seams.

Clear ruler—essential for measuring "gauge" or the size of the actual stitches. Correct fit of garments depends on knowing the number of stitches per inch (cm) in a particular project. A six-inch ruler is long enough for this purpose. Using a clear, as opposed to a solid ruler, makes it easy to see and count the stitches being measured.

Tape measure—36" (1 m) will be sufficient for most purposes, but many crocheters use a 60" (2 m) measure for larger projects, such as afghans.

Stitch markers—anything from scraps of contrasting yarn, to safety pins, bobby pins, paper clips, commercially or custom made markers, that can be placed into a particular stitch and later removed. Avoid the solid ring markers used in knitting, as they cannot be removed from crochet without wire cutters!

Sticky notes—used for keeping track of the current row in a written pattern.

Hook gauge—this little tool identifies the exact size of hooks without labels, and hooks that have been inaccurately labeled by the manufacturer. Inline or Bates-shaped hooks can be measured with a knitting needle gauge, but tapered or Boye-shaped hooks are best measured with a V-gauge, as shown in the picture (green plastic square with cut notches), or with a small set of calipers. To measure a hook, place the round shaft of the hook, between throat and thumbrest, in the smallest space it will fully fill in the gauge. Read the measurement in millimeters or letter size for that space.

All the necessary notions can be kept in a zippered plastic bag, or any other convenient container, but it's a good idea to keep them together and handy, as they will be used often in most projects. Many commercial notions bags are available, but any appropriately sized, easy-to-open container will do just fine!

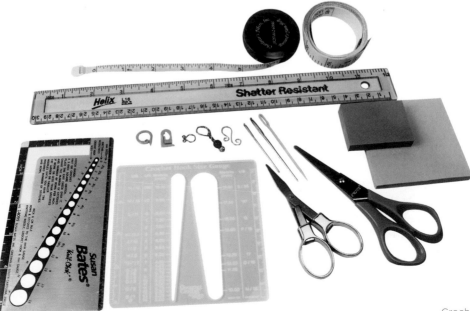

Starting to Stitch

HOW TO HOLD THE CROCHET HOOK

There is no one "right way" to hold the crochet hook, but some are more effective, efficient, and healthier for the hand and wrist than others. The three most common hook holds are the Pencil Hold, the Knife Hold, and the Chopstick Hold. Many older crochet instructions teach the traditional Pencil Hold as the only correct method. It was developed at a time when ladies wanted to appear graceful and elegant while engaged in any activity, and its primary feature is that the "pinkie" finger can easily be held at an elegant angle. However, this underhand hold requires much more movement of the wrist in every stitch, which can lead to repetitive stress injuries, such as carpal tunnel syndrome. The Chopstick Hold is similar, in that it requires constant bend in the wrist, and also places the least coordinated fingers in position to control loops of yarn on the hook. However, many crocheters continue to find one of these to be their preferred hold, and can be successful by taking extra breaks to rest the wrist, and/or wearing a supportive fingerless glove. The Knife Hold was developed more recently, in order to provide increased control of loops on the hook and increased comfort for the

Pencil Hold—hook over top of hand, between thumb and first finger

Chopstick Hold—hook over top of hand, between fingers

hand and wrist. This overhand method has gained popularity as the crafting population has grown more concerned with fun and health than with elegance. Try the different holds in the first two projects, to find the best style for your hands.

Most people will hold the hook in the right hand, and the yarn in the left hand. Because crochet uses both hands, even left-handed crocheters are not disadvantaged, and often find it a distinct advantage to hold and move the yarn, instead of the hook, with their dominant hand. However, some "lefties" do prefer to hold the hook in the left hand, and reverse for themselves all directional instructions. The photographs in this book all show the hook in the right hand, even though the pictured crocheter writes with her left! Whether to move the yarn more, or the hook more, is a personal decision, but in either case, there is an initial period of feeling awkward, regardless of hand preference!

Knife or Overhand Hold—hand over top of hook, wrist in neutral position

HOW TO HOLD THE YARN

There is also no one "right" way to hold the yarn, and each crocheter goes through a process of experimentation to find a satisfactory balance between firm control and necessary flow as the yarn is used in each stitch. The photos here show three common, effective methods. Notice that in each, the index finger is extended, ready to move the yarn where needed, and that other fingers regulate the tension or flow of the yarn as it is used.

Don't be afraid to experiment, and don't expect to settle on a yarn hold in the first few projects! It takes time and repetition for fingers and yarn to become accustomed to working together.

"Woven" yarn hold: Yarn from the working ball simply passes over and under alternate fingers. Tension is increased by squeezing fingers together when needed.

Simple "fist" hold: Yarn from the working ball is held in the fist. Tension is increased by closing the fist.

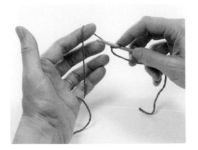

Looped tension hold: Yarn passes between pinkie and ring fingers, around pinkie and across palm, then around index finger. Tension is increased by curling the pinkie finger and holding it against ring finger.

HOW TO GET YARN ON THE HOOK—THE SLIP KNOT

All crochet begins with a slip knot. This simple knot is identical to one half of a "bow" when tying shoes. Start by making a loop, about 8" (20.5 cm) from the end of the yarn, with the yarn tail away from you, behind the circle that's been formed. Push the tail through to form a loop; tighten the loop by pulling the yarn attached to the main ball.

Place the slip knot on the hook, with the working yarn away from you.

> ### CROCHET LANGUAGE
>
> **Working yarn**—the yarn attached to the ball of yarn from which you are working. In crochet, the working yarn is always held at the back of the fabric being created.
>
> **Tail**—the short length of yarn extending from the slip knot.
>
> **Front of the work**—the side closest to you as you crochet.
>
> **Back of the work**—the side of the work facing away from the crocheter.
>
> **Right side**—the side of the fabric that will be most viewed when the project is complete. When working back and forth in rows, the right side and wrong side will alternately be facing you, and when facing you, will be called the front of the work.
>
> **Wrong side**—the side of the fabric that will be less viewed (i.e., inside of a garment) when project is complete.

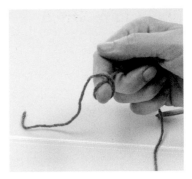

Yarn loop with tail behind.

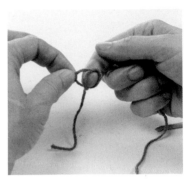

Pushing tail through to form loop.

When a slip knot is formed correctly, pulling on the tail will tighten the loop, and pulling on the working yarn will tighten the knot. Pull the tail to snug the loop to the shaft of the hook. It needs to be close enough that "daylight" doesn't show through, but loose enough to move easily up and down the shaft of the hook. Use the index finger to hold that loop in place and prevent it from spinning around the hook. It may also be helpful to spend a few minutes practicing using the index finger to move the loop slightly up and down the shaft of the hook without losing control of it. Everything is now in place to make the first crochet stitch!

WHAT YOU'LL NEED

- Worsted (#4) yarn
- Crochet hook size H, I, or J (5.00, 5.5 or 6.00 mm)

THE CHAIN STITCH

1 With the chin of the hook facing you, and the right index finger holding the loop on the hook, the left hand brings the yarn over the top of the hook, from the back, and down across the throat of the hook. The left thumb and second finger pull down on the slip knot to open up a small space at the bottom of the loop on the hook, while the left index finger moves the working yarn.

2 The right hand turns the hook downward to a "6 o'clock" position, catching the wrapped yarn with the hook, and pulls it through the loop already on the hook. The finger holding the loop on the hook lets go at this point, and will take its place to control the new loop, now on the hook. DO NOT pull or tighten the stitch once completed. The chain now being formed serves as a base for the next row of stitches, and must be made loosely. To work the following row, the hook will be inserted between the threads of each chain stitch, so be sure to work loosely enough to allow insertion.

Practice making chains until it becomes a fluid motion and the resulting loops become even in their size and shape.

Pattern instructions will nearly always start with "Chain ____," with a number filling in the blank. To count chains, lay the work flat, so that the side with a flat braided or sideways Vs appearance is facing up. Each V is one stitch. All other crochet stitches will also have the sideways V at the top of every stitch, and this is what is counted to determine the number of completed stitches. Never count the loop currently

Correct direction for yarn over—hook is under yarn as yarn comes over the hook from the back, and down across the hook at the front.

Wrong direction for yarnover. If yarn is wrapped in this direction, the stitches will twist, affecting the appearance and function of the fabric.

Hook pulling yarn through loop.

Completed first chain stitch.

TIP It doesn't matter whether yarn is pulled from the outside or the inside of a ball. In either case, even tension is easier to achieve by pulling out a yard or two at a time instead of requiring the action of the hook to pull yarn from the skein for each stitch. Many crocheters prefer to pull from the inside as they work, though, since it's a simpler motion and doesn't cause the yarn ball to roll around as much.

1 2 3 4 5 6 7 8 9 10

on the hook—there was a loop on the hook before a stitch was made, and as it's replaced continually by a new loop, it is still not actually part of any stitch. Start counting with the V immediately below the hook, and stop at the last V in line before the tight knot at the end.

PRACTICE SWATCH

Make a slip knot and start chaining. Each time the loop is pulled through, a stitch is completed, and the next chain stitch starts. Gradually, try to make the chains of even size and

WHAT YOU'LL NEED

- Worsted (#4) yarn
- J (6 mm) or K (6.50–7 mm) hook

WHAT YOU'LL LEARN

- Fluency with the chain stitch
- How to fasten off finished work

large enough that the hook tip can easily be inserted into each chain.

When each length of chain is as long as you like, "fasten off

the work," thus: cut the working yarn about 8" (20.5 cm) away from the work. Use the hook to pull this tail of yarn right through the last chain stitch made. The last stitch is now locked and will not unravel. This is the way all crochet ends. Some older patterns simply say "break off yarn," but that will always imply that this fastening-off step is what's needed.

Troubleshooting

If the chain spirals or twists slightly as it grows longer, the stitches are a little too tight. "Kinking" or "elbows" in the length of chain indicate that some of the stitches are looser and others tighter than their neighbors. It's better to work toward making them all a bit looser. A tight chain may appear tidy or elegant, but will cause frustration and difficulty later, when the hook must be inserted into those stitches.

Top to bottom: ideal tension, tension too tight, uneven tension

PROJECT 1: "Chain Gang" Boa

Here's a fashion statement crocheted entirely in chain stitch! Whether you make the plain or beaded version, this fun and quick scarf will be a great addition to any accessory wardrobe.

WHAT YOU'LL LEARN. . . . .

- Fluency with the slip knot and chain stitch in different combinations of hook and yarn

- How to weave in yarn ends securely at the finishing stage of a project

WHAT YOU'LL NEED . . . .

YARN

- Less than 1 skein each (25 yds [23 m]) or so) of 5 to 7 different yarns, a mix of light worsted (#3), worsted (#4), and chunky (#5) in your choice of fiber. Plain textured yarns will be better than slubby or haloed yarns. Choose colors that coordinate and please you

HOOKS

- H, I, and J (5.00, 5.50, and 6.00 mm)

NOTIONS

- Scissors
- Large-eyed yarn or darning needle
- Measuring tape or yard stick

1 Arrange the yarns in three groups, according to visible thickness. The H (5.00 mm) hook will be used with the thinnest group, the I (5.50 mm) hook with the mid-sized group, and the J (6.00 mm) hook with the thickest yarns.

2 Leaving a 6" to 8" (15 50 20.5 cm) tail, make a slip knot in one of the thin (Group A) yarns. Place the loop on the H (5.00 mm) hook and snug it to a natural fit.

3 Make 100 chain stitches, trying for a loose, even size to the loops. Don't worry if the chain seems to twist; it's normal and only means the work is a little on the tight side. Work toward even tension or gauge. Measure the length of the chain, laid flat but not stretched. Don't count the beginning tail in your measurement, only the chain itself. Somewhere between 22" to 26" (56 to 66 cm) indicates the correct size of each stitch.

4 Continue to chain until the chain is approximately 72" (1.85 m) long. (About 280-300 stitches, but this is a general guideline; accurate counting is not necessary.)

(continued)

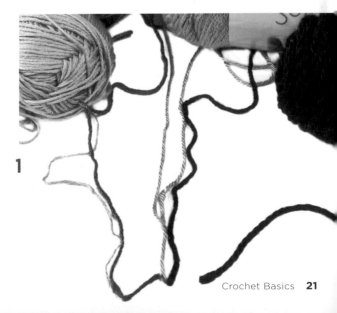

1

PROJECT 1: "Chain Gang" Boa
(continued)

5 Fasten off: cut the yarn, leaving a 6" to 8" (15 to 20.5 cm) tail, and pull the tail through the last chain loop made.

6 Repeat steps 2 to 5 with the H (5.00 mm) hook and the other Group A yarns, until there are 2 to 4 separate pieces of chain, each measuring about 72" (1.85 m) long.

7 With the I (5.50 mm) hook and yarns from the mid-sized group, Group B, repeat steps 2 to 5. Because the hook and yarn are larger, the gauge will be different for this group. The 100 chains should measure between 30" to 33" (76 to 84 cm). About 225 to 235 total chain stitches will make the 72" (1.85 m) length. Repeat with the yarns from Group B, until you have 2 to 4 Group B lengths of chain.

8 Using the J (6.00 mm) hook and the thickest group (Group C) of yarns, repeat steps 2 to 5. Gauge with this hook and yarn combination will yield a gauge measurement of about 100 stitches = 32" to 34" (81.5 to 86.5 cm). The 72" (1.85 m) length of completed chain stitches will consist of about 210 to 220 stitches. Repeat this step at least once, so there are two or more chains made with Group C yarns.

TIP If, in spite of careful math and measurement, one or more of the chains turns out more than a couple of inches longer than the rest, it's easy to adjust the length at this point. Gently pull the fastened yarn tail back through the last stitch, and pull out the last few stitches made, till the piece is approximately as long as all the others. A slight variation (1" to 2" [2.5 to 5 cm]) in the lengths of chain will enhance the final project, but one significantly longer chain will detract.

9 There are now seven to eleven lengths of chain, in various thicknesses, each about 72" (1.85 m) long. Weave in both tails of each chain, as follows: Thread one tail onto the darning needle; sew in and out of chain loops, working up the chain, for about 2" (5 cm).

10 Reverse direction and sew in and out, being careful not to "un-do" the first line of stitches, working back toward the end of the chain. Cut the tail with scissors, close to the end of the chain, and give a slight tug to tighten the remaining bit of tail. The tug will pull the last bit of tail inside the end of the chain. Repeat for opposite end of chain, and for each end of all chains.

11 Tie a simple overhand knot in each end of each chain length, as close to the end as possible, and tug it tight. The resulting chains will all be of slightly different lengths.

12 Fold each chain length in half and mark the center. (This is easily done by tying all the chains together temporarily, at their centers, with a contrasting piece of yarn.)

13 With the centers of all chains together, tie an overhand knot (one loop and pull the end through) near each end, so that 3" to 6" (7.5 to 15 cm) of all the chains remain beyond the knot. All chains are now joined together at each end.

14 Tie another knot half-way between each end-knot and the marked center. Remove center marker.

VARIATION

Try variations on the Chain Gang! Use different combinations of yarn, and different numbers of chains. Add a bead or button to each end of each chain just before weaving in the tail. (Be sure to purchase beads with a large enough center hole to accommodate yarn needle and yarn.)

CROCHET LANGUAGE

Most crochet patterns are written in a shorthand of standard abbreviations. A list of all these common abbreviations appears on page 186. Here is what a standard pattern for the Chain Gang Boa would look like:

Chain Gang Boa

Materials
Yarn
25yds each of 5-7 different yarns, mixed light worsted, worsted and chunky
Shown:Group A
Naturally Caron "Spa" (75% Microdenier Acrylic, 25% Bamboo; 3 oz/251 yds) color 0005 Ocean Spray
Naturally Caron "Country" (75% Microdenier Acrylic, 25% Merino Wool; 3 oz/185 yds) color 0013 Spruce

Group B
Caron "Simply Soft" (100% Acrylic; 6 oz/315 yds) color 0005 Blackberry
Caron "Simply Soft Party" (99% Acrylic, 1% Metallic; 3 oz/164 yds) color 0007 Black Sparkle

Group C
Caron "Simply Soft Chunky" (100% Acrylic; 5 oz/160 yds) color 0007 Wine Country
Hooks: H, I, and J (5.00, 5.50, and 6.00mm)
Notions: Measuring tape, Scissors, Yarn needle, optional: 7-10 large-eyed beads or buttons

Finished size
Approximately 65" long × 3" wide (165 × 7.5 cm)
Gauge
With H hook and light worsted yarn, 100 ch = 22" to 26" (56 to 66 cm). Exact gauge is not important for this project.

Stitches and Abbreviations Used
chain = ch
stitch(es) = st(s)
approximately = approx
yard(s) = yd(s)

Note: Yarns should be sorted into groups A, B, and C, from thinnest to thickest.

Instructions
1. With H (5.00mm) hook and each Group A yarn, ch approx. 72" (185 cm) (about 280-300 sts). Fasten off. Make a total of 2-4 Group A pieces.
2. Repeat 3–5 times with I (5.50mm) hook and Group B yarns. Repeat 2-4 times with J hook and Group C yarns.
Assembly/Finishing
Weave in tails on all chains. Tie a knot at each end of each finished chain. Mark centers of chains. With centers held together, tie a knot 3-6" (7.5 to 15 cm) from each end, bundling all chains together. Tie another knot half-way from each end knot to center. Remove center marker.

CHAPTER 2: Single Crochet in Rows

One of the wonderful aspects of crochet is the number of options—such as those discussed in the last chapter for holding the hook and yarn. Options exist, too, as we begin to work stitches into the chain and build a fabric. Beginners can find the number of choices a bit overwhelming! Knowing what factors or circumstances make one choice preferable to another can help to dispel the fear of "doing it wrong."

This chapter will introduce the single crochet stitch (abbreviated "sc") and show various options for working single crochet into the chain. Then rows of single crochet stitches will be worked on top of one another to create a useful fabric. The practice swatch will help to address common errors and the project will use the new skills to make a set of thirsty, bright, and bold coasters, in a choice of different yarns and finishing techniques.

WHAT YOU'LL LEARN . . . .

- Where to insert the hook in the chain to begin stitching
- How to correctly form the single crochet stitch
- How to end one row and begin the next

WHAT YOU'LL NEED . . . .

YARN

- Worsted weight (#4) yarn

HOOKS

- Sizes I (5.50 mm), J (6.00 mm), and K (6.50 mm)

NOTIONS

- Scissors
- Yarn needle
- 2 stitch markers

The Single Crochet Stitch

Start by making a slip knot and placing it on the size K (6.50 mm) hook. Chain 11 loosely. Remove the K hook from the work and insert the J (6.00 mm) hook. Even many experienced crocheters typically make the foundation chain with a hook larger than the one that will do the actual stitching. This practice is especially helpful if there's any doubt as to whether the chain stitches are loose enough to work in, and prevents much frustration.

In naming the stitches to determine where to insert the hook, stitches are counted from the hook back toward the original slip knot. The loop on the hook is not counted, and the chain immediately below the hook is called the first chain. Single crochet rows always start with one unused chain. This provides space for maneuvering the hook as the row begins, creates an even edge to the fabric being created, and is called the "turning chain."

So to begin, locate the second chain from the hook by counting the sideways Vs on the front of the chain. This is the first space in which to work a single crochet stitch. Each chain consists of 3 strands: the lower or front arm of the V is called the Front Loop; the upper or back arm of the V is the Back Loop, and the central strand, best seen from the back of the chain, is usually called the Bottom Bump or Back Bar. The first choice to make is exactly where to insert the hook. In one sense it really doesn't matter, and successful fabric can be created by inserting the hook at any point in each chain! But there are some factors to keep in mind. It's easiest to insert the hook right into the middle of the chain, under the Back Loop and over the other two threads. This method starts the project quickly and easily, but stretches each chain stitch out, leaving a hole and sometimes making it difficult to see the next chain in line. If an edging will later be worked or if the pattern directs that later work will also be started in the opposite side of the chain, then this method is entirely appropriate; although it may take a bit of practice to be confident in finding the next adjacent chain.

Many beginners find it the only practical place for insertion, until their fingers become more dexterous at manipulating yarn and hook. Inserting the hook only under the lower edge, under the Front Loop, has the same effect.

Inserting the hook under only one loop both stretches out a hole, making that chain larger than its neighbors, and also creates a fabric edge without "finished" appearance, and the item will need an edging. On the other hand, inserting the hook under two of the strands, whether under the Front and Back Loops, or under the Back Loop and Bottom Bump, will not stretch out the stitch. The resulting edge will probably need an edging in order to appear the same as the opposite end of the piece of fabric.

The third option is to turn the chain over and insert the hook under the Bottom Bump. This method is a little trickier at the start, but creates a completely finished edge, identical to the one that will exist at the other end of the work, where the tops of stitches form the edge.

(continued)

Insertion under Front Loop only.

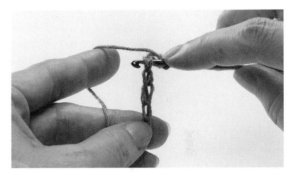
Insertion under Front and Back Loops.

Insertion under Back Loop and Bottom Bump.

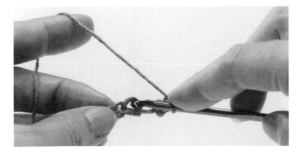
Insertion under Back Loop only.

Insertion under Bottom Bump only.

The Single Crochet Stitch (continued)

For the purpose of this lesson, it's more important to consistently locate each chain and make just one stitch in it, than to insist on one particular insertion.

1 Insert the hook into the second stitch from the hook, by poking the tip in, from front to back, moving the tip of the hook away from you. Make sure not to insert the hook from back to front of the work, as that will cause twisting of stitches and make succeeding rows more and more difficult to work.

2 With the hook now at the back of the work, and the working yarn being held at the back by the left hand, the hook will be located just beneath the working yarn. Catch the working yarn with the chin of the hook, and pull that new loop toward you through the work, to the front. This step is commonly abbreviated as "yo and draw up a loop." There are now two loops on the hook.

3 Yarn over just as in making chains, and pull the new loop through both of the loops on the hook. This step is abbreviated as "yo and pull through 2." One single crochet stitch is now complete. It consists of two vertical "feet" in

Yarn over at back of work.

Loop drawn up, 2 loops on hook.

Hook pulling yo through 2 loops.

Completed single crochet stitch, arrow shows location of next chain stitch in line.

the chain, and a new Front Loop and Back Loop at its top.

4 Locate the next chain, immediately to the left of the stitch just completed. Repeat steps 1 to 3 to form the next single crochet stitch.

5 Continue in this manner until each chain has one single crochet stitch in it. There should be 10 single crochets, and they are counted, same as chains, by looking at the braided top edge of the work. The tops of the stitches appear just like a row of chain—a series of sideways Vs. Count the stitches to make sure that there are 10.

Completed first row of 10 single crochet (sc) stitches.

Troubleshooting

If there are fewer than 10 stitches it means that one or more chains were missed or skipped. These may appear as holes or spaces between the bases of the single crochet stitches.

On the other hand, if there are more than 10 stitches, it means that two or more stitches have been worked into the same chain. These can be located by finding single crochets crowded together, with their "feet" angled instead of straight. Also, the row will bend like an elbow wherever two or more stitches are worked in the same chain. (This characteristic will actually be very useful, later, in creating different shapes with crochet.)

If you have more or fewer than 10 stitches, use the troubleshooting photos to locate the problem. Remove the hook from the final loop and gently pull stitches out, just back to the spot where the problem occurred. Stick the hook back into the top of the last "good stitch," and begin working again.

Missed or skipped chains result in fewer stitches, spaces between stitches, and the work bends upward at the ends.

Working more than one single crochet (sc) in a chain (ch) results in more than 10 stitches in the row and causes the work to bend downward.

TIP The most difficult row, for most crocheters, is the first one, working into the chain. There is little to hold on to, and the stitches are less visually obvious. Take your time with this step and remember to work loosely, so there is room to insert the hook into the tops of the stitches of Row 1 when you get to Row 2.

Array of possible stitch markers.

Ready to start Row 2, blue marker is first stitch made in Row 1.

TURNING THE WORK

Before beginning Row 2, where single crochets will be worked in the tops of the stitches of Row 1, there are two small things that must happen: the work needs to be turned so that the unworked tops of Row 1 stretch out to the left, and one chain (the "turning chain") needs to be worked. Many beginners also find it useful to place a stitch marker in the top of the first stitch worked in each row.

Look at the row just completed and place a marker in the first stitch you made. The marker can be slipped onto the front or the back loop of the top of the stitch, at the opposite (beginning) end of the row from where the hook is now situated. Also mark the last stitch, the one most recently completed. The first stitch of the following

row will be made in this marked stitch, then work in every stitch including the marked stitch at the other end of the row.

Marking helps to make sure every stitch in every row is worked. It doesn't matter which of these (the marking, the ch1, or the turning) is done first, and patterns will specify one way or another at the convenience of the designer. Turn the work as if you were turning the page of a book, with the tops of Row 1's stitches still at the top of the work. Chain 1 (yo and pull through 1 loop), and Row 2 will begin.

ROW 2—WORKING SC INTO SC

As before, the loop on the hook will not count. The loop immediately below the hook is the turning chain. Locate the first actual stitch of the row, immediately below or to the left of the turning chain. Insert the hook under both the front and back loops. It is possible to work under only one of

Correct hook insertion into a sc.

the loops, but that's a different stitch and creates a different texture to the fabric. The standard way to work all basic crochet stitches is to insert under both loops of the top V. When a pattern intends that only one loop is used, that will be clearly stated.

Complete one sc stitch in each stitch across the row. The three steps of each stitch are the same as for the first row, except that most people find it easier to work into sc stitches than into chains!

PRACTICE SWATCH

Using the same hook and yarn, follow this pattern, written in standard pattern language. If necessary, refer to previous "Quick Reference" explanations to help in understanding pattern language:

Foundation: Ch 13.

Row 1: Sc in 2nd ch from hook and in each ch across row. Turn.

Rows 2–8: Ch 1, sc in each st across. Turn. At end of Row 8, fasten off.

Finishing: Weave in tails. (This is the same process used to sew in the tails in the Chain Gang Boa project—simply thread the tail onto a yarn needle and run it through the inside of a row in one direction, then vertically through two or three rows, then opposite to the first direction in another row.)

WHAT YOU'LL NEED . . . .

- Worsted yarn
- J (6.00 mm) hook
- Yarn needle

GAUGE

- Exact gauge is not important for this project

STITCHES AND ABBREVIATIONS USED

- chain = ch
- single crochet = sc
- stitch(es) = st(s)

TIP Count rows by looking for the definite horizontal lines. In the finished swatch photo, there are two rows of sc between each horizontal line. Counting is easiest to do with the right side of the first row worked facing up, because the first horizontal line will appear at the top of Row 2, and another after every even-numbered row. When looking at the wrong side of the first row, the first horizontal line is at the top of Row 1, and the lines appear after every odd-numbered row. To mark the right side of Row 1, slip a stitch marker through the front legs of any stitch in that row, as it faces you as its being worked.

Troubleshooting

It's normal for small swatches of single crochet to curl diagonally, from the lower right corner and the upper left corner. This is due to the shape of the stitch. Because curling is more pronounced if the work is a little tight, one way to minimize curling is to work loosely. Most projects will also call for an edging to be worked around the outside of single crocheted pieces, or for seams. Either of these finishing steps usually eliminates the curling. Blocking finished work is another way to flatten it, and will be discussed in detail in a later chapter.

Normal curling of edges.

PROJECT 2: Bright and Bold Coasters

VERSION A: DOUBLE LAYER COTTON/HEMP

These coasters can be made of either cotton or cotton/hemp blend. Acrylic yarn does not absorb liquid, so is less useful for coasters. The crochet will be worked at a tighter gauge, to provide a stiff, solid fabric, capable of protecting furniture. Each coaster is made from two layers of crochet fabric joined together with crocheted edging.

WHAT YOU'LL LEARN...

- How to read a pattern with several steps
- How to measure and adjust gauge
- How to attach a new yarn and work single crochet edging, including corner increases
- How to join two stitches with a slip stitch
- How to finish a project with steam blocking

WHAT YOU'LL NEED...

- For set of 4 coasters

YARN

- Light worsted (#4) cotton or cotton/hemp blend yarn, about 100 yds (92 m) each, in 3 colors
- Shown: Plymouth Yarns "Grass" (65% Cotton, 35% Hemp; 50g/115 yds) , 9086 Red (A), 9072 Aqua (B), 9089 Multi (C).

HOOK

- Size G (4.25 mm) or size needed to match gauge

NOTIONS

- Yarn needle
- Stitch markers (optional)

FINISHED SIZE

- Approximately 4½" wide by 4" tall (11.5 × 10 cm)

GAUGE

- 15 stitches = 3½" (9 cm), 14 rows = 3¼" (8.5 cm). Exact gauge is not necessary for this project

STITCHES AND ABBREVIATIONS USED

- chain = ch
- single crochet = sc
- slip stitch = sl st
- stitch(es) = st(s)

INSTRUCTIONS

Note: Stitch counts are listed in {brackets} at the end of row instructions.

For each coaster make one square with A and one with B.

Foundation: Ch 16.

Row 1: Sc in 2nd ch from hook and in each ch across. Turn. {15 sc}

Row 2: Ch 1, sc in each st across. Turn. {15 sc}

Rows 3–14: Repeat Row 2.

At end of Row 14, measure the row gauge. Flatten your piece and measure to see whether it's larger or smaller than the stated 3¼" (8.5 cm) tall. If the difference is more than ¼" (6 mm), you may want to work an extra row, pull out a row, or accept that your coaster is unique and slightly different from the designer's. As long as all your squares

Troubleshooting/Measuring Gauge

When Row 2 is complete, flatten the work without stretching and use a tape measure to check whether your 15 stitches measure 3½" (9 cm). If your row is less than 3½" (9 cm) wide, your stitches are tighter than the designer's and you should change to the next larger hook size. If your row is more than 3½" (9 cm) wide, your stitches are looser than the designer's and you should change to the next smaller hook size. By taking time to match gauge, you ensure that your project ends up the correct size and shape. This is less important with a small project such as this one, but very important when making a garment to fit a particular size body! In larger projects, it's important to work a larger gauge swatch, so that the gauge can be measured on interior stitches and rows. For a project this small, simply check that number of stitches per inch (centimeter) is reasonably close over the first couple of rows.

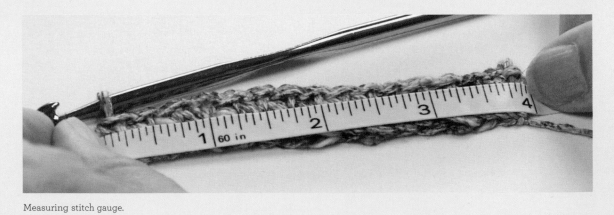

Measuring stitch gauge.

match each other, and are an appropriate size for the coaster's function, it's fine. Remember, the edging yet to be worked will add to the dimension of the squares. If you change the number of rows, the number of stitches you work in each round of the edging will change. In that case don't be alarmed when your stitch count for the edging doesn't match the given count! When satisfied with the size and shape of the square, fasten off, leaving a tail to weave in. Weave in beginning and ending tails.

Assembly/Edging

Make a slip knot with C and place it on the hook. Attach to the work thus: hold the two completed squares together with Row 14 of each square at the top, so the sideways Vs at the tops of the stitches have their "points" facing to the left. Insert the hook through both squares at the center of Row 14. The hook will go under the front and back loop of one A stitch and one B stitch.

Work a sc stitch by catching the working (C) yarn at the back and drawing up a loop, then completing the stitch as usual. In patterns, this step is described as, "Attach yarn C with a sc at center of row 14 of both squares, working through both thicknesses."

Three sts in corner.

Edging Round 1: Work 1 sc through both thicknesses of each stitch until the corner of the piece. In corner stitch (last stitch of row 14), work 2 more sc in the same space. (Total of 3 sc in corner st. This "increase" allows the work to progress around the corner of the square.)

Now working down the side of the squares, continue to insert the hook through both thicknesses, working 1 sc in each row end, (from Row 14 to Row 1) to the next corner. Always insert the hook so that at least two strands of the row end are above the hook, to avoid stretching out the stitches. Some crocheters prefer to insert the hook under the entire end stitch of the row; some prefer to insert the hook into the side of the end stitch with two strands above the hook. It's a matter of personal preference, so try it both ways for a few stitches to see which appearance you like best. Then remove the stitches in the "other" method, and continue with the chosen method. The photograph shows insertion into the center of the row end stitches.

Hook inserted under four strands, to include a stitch from each square.

(continued)

Working in row ends.

Joining end of round to beginning, with a slip stitch (sl st).

At next corner, work a corner increase (3 sc in same stitch). Now work along the bottom edge, inserting the hook under the remaining, unworked loop or loops of the foundation chain, through both thicknesses, matching stitches of the two squares. Work 1 sc in each ch across to corner.

Work a corner increase, in last unworked loops, then work along the row ends of Rows 1–14, as

before, to final corner. Work final corner increase in the end of Row 14, then 1 sc through both thicknesses in each st to beginning of Round 1. Join the last stitch made to the first with a sl st, thus:

Insert hook under both loops of first sc, yo and pull loop through BOTH the work AND the loop on the hook, slip stitch completed.

Chain 1. Turn. {Round 1 = 62 sc, not counting slip stitch or chain}

Round 2: *Sc in each sc to corner, 3 sc in center st of corner; repeat from * 3 more times, sc in each remaining st of final side; join with a sl st. Fasten off.

Working in opposite side of chain.

CROCHET LANGUAGE

An asterisk always lets you know that a section of directions will be repeated. Follow the directions and then repeat the designated number of times by going back to the * each time you complete the direction. If directed to "repeat from * across" or "repeat from * around," then do the repeated portion over and over to the end of the current row or round.

Finishing

Weave in yarn tails, leaving final end in the space between the two joined squares. When all four coasters are complete, steam block them.

STEAM BLOCKING TO FINISH A PROJECT

Steam blocking is a method recommended for yarns made primarily from plant fibers or synthetics, but not for wool, silk, or alpaca. Blocking methods for those fibers will be discussed later. In general, blocking is any means used to help all the stitches relax into one another, to even the tension of all the stitches, and to make the finished fabric lie flat at its correct dimensions. To block your coasters with steam, cover an ironing board or other flat surface with a terry cloth towel. Lay the coasters on the towel and use fingers to shape them into nice squares. Pin in place if they seem prone to shifting, but pinning is optional.

Lay a dampened towel over the coasters. Set the iron to its highest dry temperature setting. The moisture in the top towel will provide a more even steaming than the steam jet of the iron could. Set the hot iron gently down on the dampened upper towel. Hold in place till steam stops rising, move to the next section of towel and repeat. Pressure is not necessary, as the weight of the iron will be sufficient. Merely hold the iron in place, allowing steam to work through the towel to the coasters. When all coasters have been steamed, turn off the iron and remove the top towel. Allow the coasters to cool and dry in place. Pins can be removed and coasters are ready to use when they are cool and dry to the touch.

TIP The two towels are important for two reasons: they protect the texture of the crocheted fabric from becoming too flattened; and they protect the yarn from scorching in the iron's heat. Never touch a hot iron directly to crocheted fabric, regardless of fiber content!

PROJECT 2: Bright and Bold Coasters

VERSION B: FELTED WOOL FOR HOT MUGS

This variation of the basic coaster pattern is made with wool yarn. Wool is absorbent, easy to work with, and especially good at insulation, making woolen coasters ideal for protecting wooden surfaces that could be damaged by the heat of winter's cider, cocoa, and coffee mugs. The crochet will be worked more loosely and the larger, somewhat limp and floppy coasters will then be felted in finishing, which shrinks the fabric, makes it very solid, and makes most stitching errors "disappear." Felting is the process of using a combination of heat, friction, and moisture to create a thick, dense, non-raveling fabric from animal fibers. Wool and mohair are the best fibers for felting. (However, yarns labeled "superwash" have been treated to resist felting, and should not be used for projects where felting is desired.)

WHAT YOU'LL LEARN

- How to read a pattern with several steps
- How to measure and adjust gauge (see Quick Reference in Version A)
- How to attach a new yarn and work single crochet edging, including corner increases
- How to join two stitches with a slip stitch
- How to finish a project by felting

WHAT YOU'LL NEED

- For set of 4 coasters

YARN

- 1 skein or ball each of two colors of 100% wool, worsted weight yarn, such as Cascade 220 or Paton's Classic Wool. Sample made with Cascade 220 (100% Wool; 100g/ 220 yds), color 7803 (A), and color 8902 (B)

HOOK

- Size I (5.5 mm) or hook needed to obtain correct gauge

NOTIONS AND SUPPLIES

- 3 tennis balls or two old pillowcases

- Top loading (standard agitation) washing machine with hot water setting

GAUGE

- Before felting, 15 sc = 4¾" (12 cm); 15 rows = 4¼" (11 cm). Exact gauge is not necessary for this project

STITCHES AND ABBREVIATIONS USED

- chain = ch
- single crochet = sc
- slip stitch = sl st
- stitch(es) = st(s)

INSTRUCTIONS

Notes

1. Crochet for a felting project needs to be done at a looser gauge than other crochet. Be sure to stitch loosely for this project.

2. Stitch counts follow row directions, in {} brackets.

3. An asterisk * denotes the beginning of an instruction that will be repeated. Follow the instructions and then return to the * to repeat, as many times as instructed.

Make one square for each coaster. For a set of four coasters, make two squares with A and two with B.

Foundation: Ch 16.

Row 1: Sc in 2nd ch from hook and each ch across. Turn. {15 sc}

Rows 2–4: Ch 1, sc in each st across. Turn. {15 sc}

When Row 4 is complete, check gauge: flatten the piece without stretching and use a tape measure to check that your piece is 4¾" wide. If it's smaller, change to a larger hook and start again. If it's up to about ¼" larger, don't worry; felting will make it come out right. If the piece is considerably wider than the stated gauge, change to the next smaller hook size and start again.

Rows 5–15: Repeat Row 2. {15 sc}.

When Row 15 is complete, measure the height of the piece. Because of the way felting works on

Finished wool square.

the structure of the stitches, the square should be slightly wider across the rows than it is tall. If the piece measures significantly different than the 4¼" stated measurement, you may choose to work an extra row, pull out a row, or accept that your coasters are unique and different from the designer's. Felting will shrink the total size, so the finished crochet square, before edging, does need to be as large as the total desired finished size. When the size is satisfactory and the square is slightly wider than tall, fasten off, leaving the yarn tail hanging.

Edging

Each square made with A will be edged with B, and each B square will be edged with A.

Hold the square so that Row 15 is at the top, with the points of the sideways Vs of the stitch tops facing to the left. Make a slip knot in the other color of yarn and place on the hook. Insert hook under both front and back loops of the center stitch of Row 15 and draw up a loop. Complete a sc with the edging color (new yarn joined to work).

Round 1: Work 1 sc in each st to the corner (last stitch in Row 15). Work 2 more sc in that same stitch, for a total of 3 sts in the corner st. This increase allows the work to lie flat as it continues around the corner. (See photo in Version A instructions.) Now working in the sides of stitches at the end of each row, work 1 sc in each row end. It's a matter of personal preference whether to insert the hook between the last stitch of a row and the previous one, or to insert into the center of each stitch. Just make sure that at least 2 strands of yarn are above the hook at the point of insertion, to avoid stretching a hole in the work. The photo above in Version A shows insertion into the row end stitches, the author's personal preference. Feel free to try both methods and choose the one with the most pleasing appearance. When the next corner is reached, work a corner increase (3 sc in the corner stitch). Now working across the bottom of the square, insert the hook under the unworked loop(s) of the foundation chain, making 1 sc in each st across. Work a corner increase at the corner and continue with 1 sc in each row end to the final corner. Work the final corner increase and then 1 sc in each st to the last unworked st where the edging color was joined. Join the last stitch of the round to the first with a slip stitch (sl st) as follows: insert hook in both loops of firstfirst st of round. Yarn over and pull through both the work and the loop on the hook at the same time. (See photo in Version A instructions). Turn.

Round 2: Ch 1, *sc in each sc to corner, 3 sc in center stitch of corner; repeat from * 3 more times, sc in each remaining st across to beginning of round; join last st to first with a sl st. Fasten off, leaving yarn tail hanging.

Finishing by Felting

Each tiny hair of the sheep's wool has microscopic barbs or hooks lining its sides. When wool fabric is exposed to the combination of heat, moisture, and friction the fabric shrinks, the barbs catch on one another, and the result a very thick and solid fabric called felt. Felt will not ravel when cut, is a great insulator, and prevents moisture from dripping through to the table below. The solid nature of felt fabric means that many slight stitching mistakes simply "disappear" in the shrinking process, so it's ideal for beginner projects in which all stitches are not yet of uniform size and shape. Creating felt is an easy way to finish a crocheted project, as long as the piece is intentionally made about ¼ to ⅓ larger than the desired finished measurement, to account for shrinkage.

Begin by setting a kettle of water to boil on the stove, at least a quart or two. Next, place the edged coasters in a top loading washing machine, along with two or three tennis balls or a couple of old pillowcases (either of these will help create the necessary friction). Set the washer for a small load at the hottest available wash temperature, add a very little detergent, and start the wash cycle. As soon as the kettle on the stove boils, add that boiling water to the washing machine. This is often necessary because most home water heaters are not set at a high enough temperature to complete felting in one cycle. Allow the wash cycle to complete, but stop the washer just before the spin. Using a large spoon, lift each coaster out of the hot water to examine it. It should have a thick, stiff appearance, and the definition of the individual stitches should have nearly disappeared into a solid sheet of felt. If not, the process can be completed at this point by hand. Grip the coaster firmly in two hands, using gloves if needed to avoid scalding, and scrub the hands together vigorously. Shift position and continue. The felting will complete "before your eyes." Drop the coaster back into the hot water and repeat with the next one. Some colors of yarn, and some brands of yarn felt more quickly and easily than others, depending on the chemicals that have been used to treat the wool. When all coasters are solid and thick, allow the washer to complete the spin and rinse parts of the cycle. Remove the coasters, lay them flat on a towel, pinch and stretch into nice squares with your fingers, and allow them to dry. The yarn tails will appear a bit like colored spaghetti noodles, but don't worry; they'll be trimmed off in the next step.

When the coasters are dry, they are ready for trimming. First, cut off all yarn tails as close as possible to the surface of the felted square. If the felt has more fuzz on the edges and surfaces than desired, this can also be trimmed with scissors or shaved with a regular hand razor. If corners are not even, they can be trimmed to "square" with scissors, but trim carefully—what's cut off can NOT be replaced! Coasters are ready for use when trimmed to satisfaction.

Felted coasters, before and after trimming.

CHAPTER 3: Single Crochet in Rounds

Many crochet projects work best when worked "in the round." This method starts at the center of a shape and works outward in concentric rounds, just like the edging rounds of the previous chapter's Bright and Bold Coasters.

Crochet in the round is used for making hats, motifs, and many other items not rectangular in shape. The single crochet stitch is the same, but every round must contain the right number of increases to maintain the desired shape (flat, curving and tubular are common shapes created by crochet in the round). The last stitch in a round connects in one of two ways with the beginning, before the next round begins. Joined rounds are the method used for the coaster edging in the last chapter. Joined rounds can be worked with turns, as in that project, or with the right side of the work facing all the time. In either case, joined rounds, like rows, always have a chain at the start, to create the height of the new stitches.

"Working in spiral," on the other hand, does not use either the slip stitch join or the starting chain. Instead, the first stitch of a new round is worked directly into the top of the first stitch of the previous round. Each method has its own advantages and limitations, which make some projects ideal for one method and some for the other. Chapters 3 and 4 present projects using the two different beginning methods for crocheting in the round. Each of the methods for ending/beginning rounds will be used as well in making the Roll Brim Cloche hat and the Phunky Phlowered Phone Carrier. We'll start by exploring consistent increases for shaping, by making a flat circular disc as a practice swatch.

WHAT YOU'LL LEARN...............

- How to start from a ring
- How to space increases to make a flat circle
- How to work joined rounds with and without turning
- How to work spiral rounds
- How to recognize beginning and ending of rounds, and keep track of stitch count

WHAT YOU'LL NEED................

YARN

- Worsted weight (#4)

HOOK

- Size H (5.00 mm), I (5.50 mm), or J (6.00 mm)

NOTIONS

- One stitch marker

Practice Swatch—Flat Circle, Starting with a Ring

Start by making a slip knot and placing it on the hook. The ring will be made by creating a chain and then using a slip stitch to join the last chain to the first one made. The number of chains made to start the ring will depend on how large a hole is desired at the center of the finished piece. A hat, for instance, or the top of a doll's head, will need to be solid, without a visible hole. On the other hand, the center of an afghan square or lace tablecloth might need the open space as part of its decorative texture. Generally, a chained ring will easily hold twice as many stitches as the number of chains. Each finished shape is based on a number of stitches that "works" with its geometric construction. For instance, a circle consists of 360 degrees, geometrically. That means that the number of stitches in each round should be a factor of 360—multiples of six work very well. A closed center needs to have the smallest possible multiple of six, six stitches, in Round 1, then. Knowing that the ring holds twice its stitches leads to the conclusion that the ring should start with three chains. However, a chain of only three, joined into a ring, makes it quite difficult to see the center of the ring, and misplacing the Round 1 stitches can be frustrating. A ring of four chains will still close up as the bases of the Round 1 stitches fill it, but will be easier to see and work into.

Chain 4 and join with a slip stitch, thus: insert the hook under 2 strands of the 4th ch from the hook (the first chain made, not the slip knot). Yarn over and pull that loop through the chain and through the loop on the hook, at the same time. Joining slip stitch (sl st) made.

Round 1: Ch 1 to start. This round will be worked by inserting the hook into the hole at the center of the ring, NOT by inserting the hook into the individual chains. This is called "working in the ring." Work 6 sc into the ring. Directions in a standard pattern will read, "6 sc in ring."

It may be necessary, as you work around the ring, to stop after every couple of stitches and slide the completed stitches to the right, so that the ring itself is still visible to the left of the hook and so that the stitches don't overlap each other.

TIP When making chains for a joined ring, work more tightly than normal. The hook will not be inserted into the actual stitches, so tightness won't be a problem. Tight chains make the center of the ring more obvious.

Join final sc to first sc of the round with a sl st, in the same manner as the chains were joined in the foundation. Turn the work, just as in turning work in rows, so that the back side of Round 1 faces you.

As the circle progresses, each round must contain six increase stitches (stitches worked in the same place as another stitch) in order to keep the circle flat. This is a "rule of thumb" or formula for creating circles in single crochet. The number of necessary increases will be different when different crochet stitches are used. When finishing each round, do not work into the joining slip stitch, or the beginning chain. All work is done in the tops of the single crochet stitches. It may be helpful to place a stitch marker in the top of the first sc of each round, as soon as that stitch is completed. Slip the marker onto the loop immediately to the right of or below the hook at the completion of the stitch.

Round 2: Ch 1, work 2 sc in the first sc and in each stitch around the circle, inserting hook under both loops, just as in working in rows. At the end of Round 2, there are 12 sc. Join with a sl st to first st of the round. Turn.

Round 3: Ch 1, *2 sc in next st, sc in next sc; repeat from * around. The asterisk lets you know that a set of directions will be repeated several times. So, start by making the ch 1, and then work 2 sc in the top of the first stitch to your left. Work only 1 sc in the next stitch. Go back to the * and keep repeating that sequence till you have worked all the way around the circle. Now there are 18 stitches in the finished round. Join with a sl st. Do not turn.

(continued)

Joining ch 4 into a ring with sl st.

Second stitch, inserting hook in ring.

Completed 3 rounds, joined and turned.

Practice Swatch (continued)

The next three rounds will be worked in joined rounds, like the first three, but without turning. This difference in method will produce a noticeably different texture in the fabric with a definite difference between the front and back, or right side and wrong side. When working into the right side (RS) of fabric, the sideways Vs at the tops of the stitches being worked in will have their points facing to the right, instead of to the left as they have when working alternating right side/wrong side rows or rounds. This may feel a bit different at first when looking for the insertion point in the top of a stitch, but is a great way to tell whether RS (right side) or WS (wrong side) of the previous row or round is facing you as you stitch.

Round 4: Ch 1, *2 sc in next sc, sc in each of next 2 sc; repeat from * around. {24 sc}. Again, this means, notice the * and be ready to come back to it. Make 2 sc in the first stich, and then 1 sc in the next, and 1 sc in the one after that. Now go back to the * and repeat the sequence over and over around the circle. There will be 24 sc in this round. End by joining with a sl st in first stitch of the round. Do not turn.

Round 5: Ch 1, *2 sc in next sc, sc in each of next 3 sc; repeat from * around. Join with a sl st in first sc. {30 sc}. In other words, start as usual with 2 sc in the first stitch of the round. Work 1 sc in each of the next 3 stitches, and then repeat the sequence around the circle, ending with 30 completed sc stitches. Join the 30th stitch to the first with a slip stitch, and do not turn.

Round 6: Ch 1, *2 sc in next sc, sc in each of next 4 sc; repeat from * around. This time, do NOT join with a sl st. {36 sc}

At this point, it's easy to see the difference in texture or surface of the two sections. The center, made from the first three joined-and-turned rounds, has an even mix between horizontal, vertical and diagonal lines in the parts of the stitches that show from either side of the work. The second section, worked from the RS without turning, looks like rings of gentle ridges on its right side, and like conjoined squares arranged in rings on the wrong side (back of the work). The next 3 rounds will have the same texture, but without the visible seam that would gradually appear if joined rounds were continued. Working in spiral, without slip stitch joins removes any visible mark where rounds end and begin. This makes for smooth shaping, but also has two other effects. It makes it difficult to keep track of the beginning of each round without a stitch marker, and it makes the beginning of the round gradually migrate in a spiral to the right, moving the distance of one stitch to the right for every round worked. Why? The top of a crochet stitch is not directly lined up over the "legs" of the stitch. This slight offset creates the spiral migration as the first stitch of each succeeding round is worked directly into the first stitch of its predecessor, without a turning or spacing chain. When working in spiral, it's essential to mark the first stitch of each round. Besides the stitch markers used so far, there is another method of marking sometimes used in this case. Cut a piece of contrasting colored yarn, 10" (25.5 cm) or so longer

Working into the tops of a RS round.

Completed 6 joined rounds.

Marking yarn shows right-diagonal "migration" of beginning of each successive round.

Troubleshooting

It's normal for a circle in which most or all of the stitches are worked without turning to "cup" just slightly, or bend inward a little at the edges. This happens because of the structure of the sc stitch, when the RS and WS are not alternated. However, if the circle bends upward a lot, and can't be pushed flat with the fingers, it means there are too few stitches in one or more of the rows. The teal circle was started with only 5 sc in Rnd 1, instead of 6. Later, the count between increases was "accidentally" lengthened, resulting in fewer than six increases in some of the rounds. The cupping is fairly severe. Rip out a cupped circle, at least to the point where it lies flat. Check the number of stitches between increases appropriate for that round, and then continue.

On the other hand, "ruffling," as in the salmon-colored circle, is a sign that there are too many stitches in one or more rounds. This circle resulted from randomly adding occasional extra increases, as well as working in the slip stitch and turning chain in the early rounds. Rip out a ruffled circle to the point where it will lie flat, and re-work, counting to place the increases correctly and being

careful NOT to crochet into the slip stitch join or the beginning chain of any round.

It will have become obvious that when all the increases are lined up with one another, the shape formed is actually a hexagon. However, a true circle can be made by simply staggering the placement of the increases from round to round. Most of the time the increase section is only a part of the whole shape, and when the rate of increase changes and the increase stitches are therefore spaced differently, the circle will "round out" and become truly round. This principle will be evident in the next project, the Roll Brim Cloche.

than you expect your whole piece to measure from center to edge. This yarn will be pulled through the first stitch in a round, and then continuously pulled through the first stitch of every successive round, forming a diagonal line across the radius of the circle. When the circle shaping is complete, the marking yarn is simply pulled out from either end.

Round 7: Insert hook under both loops of first stitch of Round 6, draw up a loop and complete the sc. Pull the marking yarn through the stitch just made. Make another sc in the same stitch. Sc in each of next 5sc, *2sc in next sc, sc in each of next 5 sc; repeat from * around. (Note that the asterisk and its repeated section are not always at the beginning of a round. When a row or round starts

differently than the normal sequence of stitches, the asterisk won't appear until the first explanation of the sequence to be repeated exactly.) {42 sc}

Round 8: Sc in marked stitch, and pull marking yarn up through stitch just made, sc in same stitch and in each of next 6 sc, * 2 sc in next sc, sc in each of next 6 sc; repeat from * around. {48 sc}

Round 9: Sc in marked stitch, and pull marking yarn up through stitch just made, sc in same stitch and in each of next 7 sc, * 2sc in next sc, sc in each of next 7 sc; repeat from * around. {54 sc}

To finish swatch, join last stitch of Round 9 to first stitch of Round 9 with a sl st. Fasten off. Remove marking yarn.

PROJECT 3: Roll Brim Cloche

This great hat gets its stripes from the use of a self-striping yarn. These yarns have a long run of each color, unlike a regular variegated or ombre yarn, in which each color runs for only a few inches before the next begins. As their name suggests, self-striping yarns are designed to automatically create stripes as the yarn from a single ball is used. The word "self-striping" will appear on the label, and will simplify the process of choosing an appropriate yarn. The pattern uses both spiral and joined/turned rounds for its shaping, and is also easy to adapt to other sizes. To make a child's hat, try using sport weight (#3) yarn and a G (4.25 mm) hook. For a baby or doll's hat, fingering (#2) yarn and an F (3.75 mm) hook will work. A man's hat can be made by using bulky (#5) yarn, a K (6.50–7 mm) hook, and leaving off the rolled brim.

WHAT YOU'LL LEARN

- How to use correct gauge to ensure fit for a wearable project
- How to shape a hat using increase rounds and "work even" rounds
- How to work "in front loop only," a single crochet variation used for shaping and texture

WHAT YOU'LL NEED

YARN

- 200 yds (184 m) of worsted (#4) wool, wool/acrylic blend, or acrylic yarn in a self-striping colorway.
- Shown: Plymouth Yarns Encore Colorspun, color 7149 (75% Acrylic, 25% Wool; 100g/200 yds)

HOOK

- Size I (5.5 mm) or hook needed to achieve gauge. Ensure proper fit by taking time to check gauge!

NOTIONS

- Yarn needle
- stitch marker

GAUGE

- Circle formed by Rnds 1–6 = 3½" (9 cm) across. Check gauge by working Rnds 1–6, then measuring diameter. If piece measures more than 3½" (9 cm) use smaller hook. If piece measures less than 3½" (9 cm) use larger hook

STITCHES AND ABBREVIATIONS USED

- chain = ch
- single crochet = sc
- slip stitch = sl st
- stitch(es) = st(s)
- round (s) = rnd(s)
- place marker in stitch = pm
- move marker to new round = mm

INSTRUCTIONS

Note: Stitch counts appear in {brackets} following instructions for the round.

Foundation: Ch 4, sl st to join in a ring.

Crown of Hat

Rnd 1: Ch 1, work 6 sc in ring, PM in first st made, and in each following rnd, MM to keep it always in first st of rnd. Do not join, work progresses in spiral. {6 sc}

Rnd 2: 2sc in each st around. {12 sc}

Rnd 3: *2 sc in next st, sc in next st; repeat from * around. {18 sc}

Rnd 4: *2 sc in next st, sc in each of next 2 sts; repeat from * around. {24 sc}

Rnd 5: *2 sc in next st, sc in each of next 3 sts; repeat from * around. {30 sc}

Rnd 6: *2 sc in next st, sc in each of next 4 sts; repeat from * around. {36 sc} Check gauge before proceeding.

Rnd 7: *2 sc in next st, sc in each of next 5 sts; repeat from * around. {42 sc}

Rnd 8: *2 sc in next st, sc in each of next 6 sts; repeat from * around. {48 sc}

Rnd 9: *2sc in next st, sc in each of next 7 sts; repeat from * around. {54 sc}

Checking gauge on Rnds 1-6.

Rnd 10: *2 sc in next st, sc in each of next 8 sts; repeat from * around. {60 sc}

Rnd 11: Sc in each st around. {60 sc}

Rnd 12: *2sc in next st, sc in each of next 9 sts; repeat from * around. {66 sc}

TIP The increase pattern changes after Rnd 10, to begin cupping the crown of the hat.

Troubleshooting

Counting rounds. When sc is worked in spiral rounds, each round appears as a ridge, a concentric ring. Starting at the center of the piece, where the first ring is Rnd 1, count the ridges straight out toward the stitch to the right of the marked stitch. This count will tell you how many rounds are complete at any moment. To keep track of rounds in the written pattern, many crocheters use a small sticky-note, and move it from row to row through the pattern's text.

Rnd 13: Sc in each st around. {66 sc}

Rnd 14: *2sc in next st, sc in each of next 10 sts; repeat from * around. {72 sc}

Rnd 15: Sc in each st around. {72 sc}

Piece is now slightly bowl shaped and measures 8½" to 8¾" across. Adjustment can be made by working extra rows, or ripping out a row if measurement is more than ¼" different.

Rnd 16: Sc in each st around. {72 sc}

Rnds 1-16 complete.

Sides of Hat (worked without increase)

Rnds 17–25: Work even (that is, 1 sc in each stitch) over 72 sts. Remember to continue to MM so that the first st of each rnd is marked as that rnd is worked. At end of Rnd 25, sl st in next st, ch 1. Turn. {72 sc}

Rnd 26 (WS): Sc in each st around; join last st to first with a sl st, ch 1. Turn. {72 sc}

Rnd 27 (RS): Sc in each st around; join last st to first with a sl st, ch 1, do NOT turn.

Rolled Brim

Now we'll use a variation of the sc stitch, single crochet in front loop only, to shape the brim.

Rnd 28 (RS): Work 1 sc flo in each stitch around; join last st to first with a sl st, do NOT turn. {72 sc}

Rnds 29 and 30: Working in both loops, and in spiral, work 1 sc in each st around. At end of Rnd 30, sl st to join last st to first, fasten off.

Finishing

Remove stitch marker(s). Use a large-eyed yarn needle to weave in both tails securely. In a later chapter, a flower pattern will be offered, which can be attached to the Roll Brim Cloche, if desired.

Working two rounds "in front loop only" creates a natural fold or roll for the hat's brim.

CHAPTER 4:
More Single Crochet in Rounds

Chapter 3 introduced crocheting in rounds by starting with a chained ring. Another way to work in the round is to start with a straight chain, as if crocheting in rows. The first "row," however, works up one side of the chain, increases at the end of the chain and then works back down the opposite side. This method is very useful for creating a seamless, sturdy bottom for many types of projects—in this case, a handy carrier for an i-Phone, Blackberry, or other mid-sized "smart-phone." Since the stitches to be used are already familiar, the new starting method, along with a new color change method, will be addressed right in the context of the project.

PROJECT 4:
Phunky Phlowered Phone Carrier

Bright and fun crocheted carriers make it easy to manage and protect our electronic devices. This phone carrier works well attached to the strap of a larger bag, and simplifies the process of locating the ringing phone, while cushioning it from bumps and bangs.

WHAT YOU'LL LEARN. . . . .

- How to work in the round from both sides of a starting chain
- How to work single crochet in back loop only for shaping
- How to follow directions with multiple repeats, using different symbols

- How to change colors in continuous stitching
- How to make a simple crocheted flower
- How to make a sturdy slip stitched tie or drawstring
- How to decrease by working two stitches "together"

(continued)

WHAT YOU'LL NEED

YARN

- About 75 yds (69 m) each of Color A and Color B, worsted weight acrylic or wool yarn. Shown: Caron Simply Soft (100% Acrylic; 6oz/315 yds) colors #9604 Watermelon (A), and #9605 Mango (B)

HOOK

- Size G (4.25 mm) or hook needed for approximate gauge

NOTIONS

- Stitch marker
- Yarn needle

FINISHED SIZE

- Instructions are for a carrier 3½" wide by 5" tall (9 × 12.5 cm), exclusive of flap and ties. A larger carrier, suitable for an e-reader device, can be made by starting with a longer chain and working more rounds to necessary size

GAUGE

- Approximately 13 stitches = 3" (7.5 cm); approximately 14 rows = 3" (7.5 cm). Exact gauge is not necessary for this project

STITCHES AND ABBREVIATIONS USED

- chain = ch
- single crochet = sc
- slip stitch = sl st
- single crochet in back loop only = sc blo
- single crochet 2 together = sc2tog (the most common way of decreasing)
- place marker = pm
- move marker = mm
- round(s) = rnd(s)
- stitch(es) = st(s)
- right side = RS (side facing as you stitch)
- wrong side = WS (side away from you as you stitch)

INSTRUCTIONS

Notes

1. Stitch counts appear in {brackets} following instructions for the round.

2. When multiple repeats are present, always work what's inside the parentheses ( ) first for the stated number of repeats and then continue with the main or asterisk (*) repeat sequence. Each time through, do the parentheses repeats first, followed by continuing the main repeat.

Foundation: With A, ch 11, loosely.

Bottom and Sides

Rnd 1: Work 3 sc in 2nd ch from hook, PM in first st made to mark beginning of rnd, sc in each of next 8 ch, 3 sc in last ch; now working in opposite side of chain, as shown in photo, sc in each of next 8 ch to complete the rnd, do not join; work proceeds in spiral. MM at beginning of each

following rnd, so that first st is always easy to locate. {22 sc}

Rnd 2: *2 sc in next st, sc in next st, 2 sc in next st, sc in each of next 8 sts; repeat from * around. {26 sc}

Rnd 3: *2 sc in next st, (sc in next st, 2 sc in next st) 2 times, sc in each of next 8 sts; repeat from * around. {32 sc}

CROCHET LANGUAGE

Start the round by making 2 sc in the first stitch. Next work the sequence inside the parentheses twice, as noted by "2 times" following the parentheses. Next make 1 single crochet in each of the next 8 stitches. Now go back to the * and repeat the entire sequence, starting with the 2 sc in one st before the parentheses, next following the instructions inside the parentheses twice, and then finishing with a single crochet in each of the last 8 stitches of the round. There are now 32 sc in the completed round, and the marked first stitch is the next stitch to the left of the hook.

TIP: Why change colors in the final loop of a stitch? The answer lies in the structure of crochet stitches. The loop that forms the top of each stitch is actually the final loop pulled through in working the previous stitch. If colors are changed at the start of a stitch, then the loop already on the hook, when it becomes the top V of the stitch, will be a different color than the other strands making up that stitch. This discrepancy would result in an uneven appearance or "jagged edge" where colors are changed. Later, when working taller stitches, consisting of more loops, colors are always changed at the point of the final "yo and pull through 2 loops" of the last stitch in the "old" color.

WS of work, bow tied of tails.

Rnd 4: Work this round in blo. (Sc blo is very similar to the sc flo used in the last chapter. In this case, begin a stitch by inserting the hook under only the back loop at the top of the indicated stitch.) Work 1 sc blo in each stitch around, stopping just before last stitch of the round.

Rnd 4 continued: In last stitch of Rnd 4, change to B, thus: insert hook as usual to begin stitch. Yarn over as usual and draw up the loop to the front of the work (two loops on hook). Yarn over with the new yarn, B, and pull through both loops on hook, leaving a tail on wrong side. Cut A, leaving a 6" tail. For security, the tails of the two yarns can

be tied together, temporarily, in a bow-knot, just like shoes. During finishing stage, the bow will be untied and each tail will be woven in to the matching-color stitches. {32 sc}

Rnds 5–22: With B and working in both loops of each st, work 1 sc in each st around. Mm to denote beginning of each round. In last stitch of Rnd 22, change to A.

Rnds 23 and 24: With A, sc in each st around. {32 sc}

Rnd 25: Sc in each of next 15 sts, ch 4, skip next 5 sts, sc in next st (ch-4 space made), sc in each of next 11 sts.

Point of insertion for single crochet in back loop only (sc blo)

(continued)

PROJECT 4: Phunky Phlowered Phone Carrier (continued)

Rnd 26: Sc in each of next 15 sts, 5 sc in ch-4 space (just like working into a starting ring; insert hook for each stitch completely under the chain, into the large hole), sc in each of next 12 sts. Do not fasten off.

FLAP

Work now proceeds in rows.

Row 1: Sc in each of next 9 sts of Rnd 26, ch 1. Turn, leaving remaining stitches of the rnd unworked. {9 sc}

Row 2: Sc in first st, sc2tog (see tip and photo), sc in each of next 9 sts, sc2tog, sc in next st, ch 1. Turn. {13 sts}

Row 3: Sc in first st, sc2tog, sc in each of next 7 sts, sc2tog, sc in next st, ch 1. Turn. {11 sts}

Row 4: Sc in first st, sc2tog, sc in each of next 5 sts, sc2tog, sc in next st, ch 1. Turn. {9 sts}

Row 5: Sc in first st, sc2tog, sc in each of next 3 sts, sc2tog, sc in next st, ch 1. Turn. {7 sts}

Row 6: Sc in first st, (sc2tog, sc in next st) twice, ch 1. Turn. {5 sts}

Row 7: Sc2tog, sc in next st, sc2tog, ch 1. Turn. {3 sts}

Rows 8–10: Sc in each st, ch 1. Turn. {3 sc}

Decrease (sc2tog).

Attachment of second yarn for flower.

TIP Remember to slide stitches to the right as you work in the ring, to prevent overlapping.

Row 11: Sc in first st, ch 10, skip next st, sc in next st (buttonloop made). Fasten off.

Flower Button

With B, leaving an 8" tail, ch 4 and join with a sl st to form ring.

Rnd 1: Ch 1, work 9 sc in ring, sl st to join last st to first.

Rnd 2: Working in front loops only, sc flo in next st, *ch 2, sc in next st; repeat from * 7 more times, ch 2, sl st in first sc. Fasten off. {9 ch-2 loops}

Rnd 3: Attach B with a sc in the unworked back loop of any stitch of Rnd 1.

All stitches of Rnd 3 are worked in remaining unworked back loops of Rnd 1. *Ch 3, sc in next st; repeat from * 7 more times, ch 3, sl st in first sc. Fasten off, leaving an 8" tail. {9 ch-3 loops}. Weave in the two shorter tails, leaving long tails to use for sewing flower to front of phone cover.

Ties

With right side facing, attach A to side of phone cover, with a sc in first unworked st of Rnd 26, beside edge of flap. Ch 45, loosely, sl st in each ch, sl st in beginning sc. Fasten off. Repeat at opposite side of flap for 2nd tie.

Finishing

Sew flower to front center of phone carrier, 8 rows below front slit. Turn carrier inside out and weave in all ends securely. Thread end of flap through front slit, so loop of flap can fit over flower for closure. Tie ties to belt loop or strap of purse, bookbag, or diaper bag.

VARIATION

Make a carrier for an e-reader or tablet device by simply lengthening the beginning chain, and correspondingly lengthening the number of stitches between increases when making the bottom and sides. Of course, more yarn will be required and more rounds will also need to be worked before the front slit and flap. The flower can also be made in any color combination and used to embellish small accessories, such as barrettes, hair ties, zipper pulls, etc. Other and larger flower/embellishment patterns will be presented in future chapters.

CHAPTER 5:
The Double Crochet Stitch

Now that the single crochet stitch is familiar, along with the methods of increasing, decreasing, working in rows and in rounds, it's time to learn the second major stitch used in crochet: the double crochet. Double crochet is a taller stitch, so every row or round worked increases the height of the fabric piece twice as fast as a row of single crochet does. Double crochet fabric is less solid, less thick, and less stiff; it drapes better and so is ideal for garments and blankets. Double crochet is also often used in combination with single crochet and other stitches to create "pattern stitches" for lace and other textures in fabric. In Chapters 5 and 6, we will explore the methods for making double crochet (abbreviated dc) stitches, and working them in rows and in rounds. The resulting projects, a soft warm neckscarf and a classic Granny Square messenger bag, will be sure to please!

WHAT YOU'LL LEARN . . . .

- How to work the double crochet (dc) stitch with correct form and tension
- How to make the correct turning chain height for rows of dc
- How to recognize and count dc stitches and rows in a project

WHAT YOU'LL NEED . . . .

YARN

- Worsted weight yarn

HOOK

- Size I (5.5 mm) or J (6 mm)

NOTIONS

- 3 stitch markers

Making the Double Crochet Stitch—Practice Swatch

Start by making a swatch of sc in rows (if a review is needed, see the Practice Swatch in Chapter 2). Work three or four rows, so there is some fabric to hold on to as the new stitch is learned. Although single crochet rows always begin with 1 chain stitch (the "turning chain"), the double crochet stitch needs a taller turning chain because it's a taller stitch. Therefore, to begin the first row of double crochet, chain 3. This is the standard turning chain for double crochet. Because the turning chain is so

tall, it will actually stand in the place of the first stitch of the row. Look at your swatch and locate the first stitch in the row. Place a marker in that stitch, and place a marker in the last of the three chains just made (chain immediately below the loop on the hook). Turn the work, to begin the row of dc.

The marked first stitch of the row will be skipped, and the first actual dc stitch of the row will be made in the stitch immediately to its left.

1 The first difference between a sc and a dc stitch is in how they are begun. The sc stitch began with insertion of the hook into the designated stitch. The dc stitch, however, begins with a yarn over (yo). This is done in the same direction as all yarn overs, back to front, right to left, with the yarn coming over the top of the hook and down in front of it.

Now insert the hook in the second stitch of the row (left of the marker), yo at the back of the work (a) and draw up a loop. There are now three loops on the hook (b).

2 Yarn over and pull that new loop through the first two loops on the hook. This step is designated "yo and pull through 2."

3 There are still two loops on the hook. Yo again, and pull the loop through the two remaining on the hook. A double crochet stitch is completed.

1A

1B

2

3

5

4 To make the second stitch, repeat steps 1–3, inserting the hook in the next stitch in the row.

Yo, insert hook, and draw up a loop.

Yo and pull through 2.

Yo and pull through 2.

5 Continue across the row, till one dc stitch stands in each sc stitch of the previous row. Now move the marker from the skipped stitch at the beginning of the row, and place it in the last stitch of the row, the last stitch made. This will be the skipped stitch at the beginning of the next row. Chain 3, mark the 3rd chain made, and turn the work.

Working Rows of Double Crochet

The second and all following rows begin in the same way as the first: with a ch-3 to turn, skipped first stitch, and then 1 dc in each stitch of the row. As soon as the first stitch of Row 2 is made, remove the marker from the skipped

(continued)

Markers shows top of turning chain and location of last stitch of Row 2.

Working Rows of Double Crochet (continued)

stitch, to use again in a few moments. When the second row is nearly complete, the last stitch of the row will be made into the marked 3rd chain of the previous row's turning chain. In this way, the number of stitches stays the same from row to row and each turning chain "becomes" a dc stitch.

Hook inserted beneath front loop and bottom bump of chain.

Completed 2nd row.

As usual, there are several ways to insert into the chain, but the best appearance of the stitch will be achieved by inserting the hook beneath the front loop and bottom bump. Since the back of that row is facing, these are the top two strands facing you as you look at the turning chain.

Counting Stitches and Rows

Like the single crochet stitches you're familiar with, each double crochet stitch has a sideways "V" at the top. When the right side of the completed stitches is facing, the Vs all point to the right. When the work has been turned and the wrong side of completed stitches is facing, the Vs point to the left. Stitches in a row can be counted by counting the Vs. However, remember that the first stitch of each row is actually the turning chain, and it has a slightly different appearance. The V is there, but is a little more difficult to see clearly. Many people find it easier to count their dc stitches by looking at the vertical part of

Troubleshooting

Most problems with double crochet in rows are caused by a few common errors. The most common mistakes are shown here, for comparison with your swatch.

Swatch on left shows the gradual increase in stitch count caused by NOT skipping the first stitch as each row begins. Swatch on right shows gradual decrease in stitch count caused by NOT working the last stitch of each row in the top of the turning ch-3.

Left—Stitches much too loose, tangling and collapsing on themselves.

Right—Stitches short and "squat," no taller than sc, caused by yanking or tugging the yarn to tighten after each "yo and pull through 2 loops" step in each stitch.

Each swatch shows 10 rows of work—4 rows of blue sc, 2 rows of pink sc, and 4 rows of green dc. Left: Right side of Row 1 is facing. Yellow pins mark tops of Rows 1, 3, 5, 7, and 9. Right: Wrong side of Row 1 is facing, pink pins mark tops of Rows 2, 4, 6, 8, and 10.

Ch 12, dc in 4th ch from hook and in each ch across.

There are now nine actual dc stitches and a ch-3 that counts as a stitch, making a total of ten stitches in the row.

the stitch, called the post. Each post has a diagonal twist on the right side, and a series of knots on the wrong side. Each post stands just below and slightly to the left of its V-shaped top. It's easy to see that the turning chain creates a vertical post like all the others in a row.

Work several more rows of dc, using the markers for last stitch in each row (first skipped stitch in the following row) and for the top of the turning chain (3rd chain made), where the last stitch of the following row will be placed. At the end of each row, count to make sure there are still ten stitches. Use the Troubleshooting box to make sure your stitches are the correct height and shape, that is, that your tension is neither too tight nor too loose. When the process becomes familiar, proceed to the second practice swatch, in which dc stitches will be worked directly into a starting chain.

Practice Swatch #2
DOUBLE CROCHET WORKED INTO CHAIN

Many projects begin with a row of double crochet stitches worked directly into the starting chain. Because each row of double crochet must start with a turning chain as tall as the stitches themselves, the beginning chain must be three chain stitches longer than the number of stitches required (for the turning chain), and then that turning chain will count as the first stitch of the first row of double crochet. This creates a net difference of two stitches. When working rows of single crochet, the length of the starting chain was one more than the desired number of stitches—eleven chains to make a swatch with ten stitches per row. To make ten stitches per row in double crochet, the starting chain will be twelve stitches.

Practice making dc in a longer chain, remembering to do a yarn over at the beginning of each stitch, before inserting the hook into the next chain. When the process is comfortable and consistent, you're ready to make Project 5, the "Longitude Scarf," which will use rows of both single and double crochet!

PROJECT 5: Longitude Scarf

With two options for fringe and bold length-wise stripes, this cozy scarf pattern makes great gifts for men, women, and kids.

WHAT YOU'LL LEARN . . . .

- How to carry yarn from one row to another when making stripes
- How to change yarn colors in double crochet
- How to attach a new ball of yarn when the ball in use runs out
- How to make two kinds of fringe
- How to combine single crochet and double crochet stitches in one project

WHAT YOU'LL NEED . . . .

YARN

- For 2-color version (shown with looped fringe), worsted weight (#4) wool or acrylic yarn, approx. 109 yds (100.3 m) of A, approx. 150 yds of B
- Shown: Valley Yarns Amherst (WEBS) (100% Superwash Merino Wool; 50g/109 yds) Olive (A), Sweet Pea (B)

HOOKS

- J (6.00 mm) and I (5.50 mm) or hooks needed to obtain gauge

NOTIONS

- Stitch markers (optional) for row ends and turning chains
- Large-eyed yarn needle

GAUGE

- In dc stitches with smaller hook, 9 sts = 3" (7.5 cm) and 2 rows = 1½" (4 cm). However, exact gauge is not necessary for this project

FINISHED SIZE

- 5½" wide by 58" long (14 × 147.5 cm), including fringe

STITCHES AND ABBREVIATIONS USED

- chain = ch
- single crochet = sc
- double crochet = dc
- slip stitch = sl st
- stitch(es) = st(s)
- yarn over = yo

INSTRUCTIONS

Notes

1. Stitch counts appear in {brackets} at the ends of rows.

2. Turning ch-3 counts as a dc at beginning of all dc rows. Turning ch-1 does NOT count as a sc at beginning of all sc rows. If necessary, mark first stitch of each row.

3. Scarf can be made longer or shorter by modifying number of ch in foundation. Add or subtract 3 ch per inch of modification desired.

TIP To count large numbers of chain stitches accurately, place a stitch marker every 25 stitches or so. Remove the markers as Row 1 is worked.

(continued)

Foundation

With larger hook and A, chain 151.

Scarf

Row 1: Change to smaller hook, sc in bottom bump of 2nd ch from hook and in each ch across. In last stitch, change to B, see explanation in Chapter 4. {150 sc}

Row 2: With B, ch 3 (in addition to loop that created color change), counting turning ch as first stitch, dc in each stitch across. {150 dc}

Row 3: Ch 3, dc in each stitch across, changing to A in last stitch. Be sure not to pull too tightly on A in the color change. Leave sufficient yarn for the "carry" to lie flat across the ends of the rows without curling the piece as it's worked. {150 dc}

TIP To change colors in a dc stitch, begin with the old color. Yo and insert hook into designated stitch, yo and draw up a loop (3 loops on hook). Yo and pull through 2 loops (2 loops remain on hook). Yo with new color and pull through both loops on hook. In a striped project, such as this one, DON'T cut the first color! Let it hang until it's needed again in a few rows. At that time, simply pick it up with the hook when ready to "yo with new color."

TIP Attaching a new ball of yarn—At some point in the project, the first ball of B is likely to be used up. When this happens, attach the new yarn just as if it were a new color: with 6″ (15 cm) or so of the old yarn remaining, work the first half of the next stitch. Finish the stitch by doing the final "yo and pull through" with the new yarn. The two yarn tails can be temporarily tied together in a bow, and woven in during finishing of the project.

Row 4: With A, ch 1, sc in each st across, ch 1. Turn. {150 sc}

Row 5: Sc in each st across. In last stitch, change to B.

Rows 6 and 7: Repeat Rows 2 and 3.

Rows 8 and 9: Repeat Rows 4 and 5.

Rows 10 and 11: Repeat Rows 2 and 3.

Row 12: Repeat Row 4. At end of Row 12, fasten off B.

Looped Chain Fringe

Row 1: With A, ch 1, rotate piece to work in row ends, sc in each sc row end and 2 sc in each dc row end (work over the strands of yarn carried from one stripe to another, to hide them). Fasten off A. At opposite end of scarf, attach A and repeat this row. {18 sc at each end of scarf}

Row 2: Sc in first st of Row 1, *ch 24, sc in next st; repeat from * across. Fasten off. Repeat at other end of scarf. {17 loops}

Finishing

Use large-eyed yarn needle to weave in all ends securely.

Variation—Three-Color Longitude Scarf with Tied Fringe

This version requires worsted weight (#4) wool or acrylic yarn, approx. 109 yds (100.3 m) each of A, B, and C. The sample was made with Valley Yarns Amherst (WEBS) (100% Superwash Merino Wool; 50g/109 yds), Soft Brown (A), Wild Rose (B), Soft Grape (C). You also need 6" (15 cm) wide piece of sturdy cardboard, or other stiff object of same width.

INSTRUCTIONS

Rows 1–12: Follow directions for Variation #1, except that Rows 6 and 7 are worked with C. At end of Row 12 of scarf, fasten off all three yarn colors, leaving 6" tails. Weave in all yarn tails securely, into rows matching colors.

Tied Fringe

Hold all 3 colors of yarn together and wrap 36 times around the piece of cardboard, small book, or other stiff object measuring 6" (15 cm) across. Do not wrap so tightly that yarn stretches, just keep it snug against the cardboard or other form. Cut yarns to separate from yarn balls. Now slide scissors under one end of the wrapped yarns and cut through. This produces 36 pieces of yarn in each color, each measuring approx. 12" (30.5 cm) long.

Insert larger hook into first row end of scarf. Catch the centers of one strand of each yarn color with hook and draw up as a loop, leaving doubled ends at back of work. Yo with all 6 strands and pull them firmly through the loop on the hook. Repeat one time in each sc row end and two times in each dc row end, across both ends of the scarf. Fringe will look best if the direction of insertion is alternated for each tuft, inserting from the RS of the work for the first tuft, WS of the work for the second, etc.

There will be some variation to the lengths of the fringe strands, inherent in the process of wrapping and tying. Lay the scarf flat and smooth out the fringe. Use scissors to cut off any strands significantly longer than the others surrounding them.

CHAPTER 6: Double Crochet Motifs in Living Color

Many crochet projects, both traditional and current, are constructed of small pieces, or motifs, attached to one another in decorative patterns, which create a highly graphic fabric. The variety in motifs, from simple to amazingly complex, is almost infinite. They are made in many shapes and sizes, can use one color or several, and can be joined to create anything from tablecloths to clothing and accessories. However, they do all have a few things in common. All motifs are worked from the center outward, and all use careful placement of the increases to create their shapes.

In this and the following chapter, we'll explore some variations and uses of the most famous of crochet motifs—the "granny square." Some people mistakenly call any square motif a "granny," but the granny square is actually a specific stitch pattern. It consists of groups of double crochet stitches (usually 3 or 4 stitches per group) separated by chain spaces. Each round is worked in the chain spaces of the previous round, and the corners are formed by working two groups of stitches and their separating space in one corner space. The granny square was very popular during the late 1960s and the 1970s, and is enjoying a resurgence of popularity in the second decade of the twenty-first century. It's one of those classic designs that cycles into "current fashion" at least once in each generation.

Chapter 6 presents the classic granny and one variation on the theme, and its project is an attractive and useful shoulder bag. Chapter 7 will further explore the uses of square motifs by joining them together to make a fun and colorful hat. So grab a familiar hook and a couple of balls of worsted yarn in colors you love, and let's get going with grannies!

WHAT YOU'LL LEARN . . . .

- How to choose colors that will "work" together
- How to make square motifs by careful placement of corner increases
- Working in chain spaces instead of in stitches
- How to make a "granny square" of any size and color sequence

WHAT YOU'LL NEED . . . .

YARN

- Worsted yarn in three colors, but choose your colors after reading through the section, "Let's Talk Color!"

HOOK

- Size H (5 mm) or I (5.5 mm)

NOTIONS

- One stitch marker

Let's Talk Color!

Many people feel insecure about their ability to choose colors for their projects. Sometimes it's a fine line between "great project" and "incredibly ugly," and it's common to fear the latter! In a sense, crocheters are painting with yarn, and that's never more true than when using multi-colored motifs. It's important to choose a palette of colors that will be pleasing to the eye when placed near each other, but how does one choose? Many crocheters simply follow the exact choices of a pattern's designer, copying the color scheme exactly—and that's a safe and reliable option, as long as your favorite colors are the same as the designer's. But copying someone else's color choice doesn't create unique and personal pieces. It means that when a lovely project is shown using a color one dislikes, the whole project might be dismissed as "ugly," although a different choice of palette would make it "beautiful." Each person has different ideas about "beautiful," but we all recognize visual harmony when we see it—we're just not confident in how to achieve it! However, an understanding of just a couple of "color theory" principles will free you to make color choices with confidence.

VALUE

When colors are removed by printing a photograph in gray scale, there are still variations—areas that are light, medium, or dark. This is the principle of "color value." In graphic designs, such as crocheted motifs, value is the first principle to consider. A design will "work" visually, if it contains contrasting values—some light areas, some medium, and some dark. It is the contrast between light and dark that keeps the eye interested in the whole piece, and allows the actual colors to be appreciated. So, when choosing yarns for a project made in motifs, make sure you choose at least one really light color and one really dark color. Any others can range between these extremes, and form the medium range.

Traditional granny square blankets used a rainbow of colors, but all the motifs in the blanket were unified by having either black or white as their outer round of work, and that same color was used to join all the motifs together and to edge the blanket. The other colors all seemed more bright and brilliant by their contrast to the black or white background. When designing your motif color scheme, it's always a safe choice to move from a light center to a dark outer edge, or vice versa. Create additional interest by re-using just a little of the center color elsewhere in the motif or in the edging of the whole project. This sudden and unexpected second contrast will delight the eye.

Each of these traditional granny squares has a light center, medium mid-section, and a dark edge for contrast. Visual unity is created by continuity in the dark area surrounding the brights.

Left to right: light, medium, and dark yarns.

Another reliable way to use value when choosing your color palette is to choose light, medium, and dark shades of the same color, which is called a "monochrome" palette.

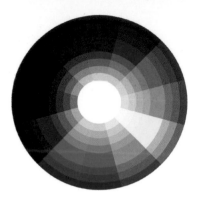

On the left, complementary colors "fight" for the eye's attention. On the right, the same colors are used in effective proportions, creating interesting visual harmony.

THE COLOR WHEEL

Because color is created by differing wavelengths of light, it's easiest to understand the relationships between colors when they are arranged in a circle called the color wheel. The color wheel is a standard artists' and designers' tool, and cardboard color wheels are available in the painting sections of craft stores as well as in specialty artist supply shops. When choosing colors for a project, a portable color wheel is a useful tool!

Most of us know that red, yellow, and blue are the "primary" colors—the colors that cannot be made by mixing others, and which are the basis for all other colors. The colors made by mixing any two of the primaries are called "secondary colors." For example, red and blue (primaries) combine to create purple (secondary); blue and yellow (primaries) combine to create green (secondary).

Complementary Colors

Looking at the color wheel, there is always a secondary color exactly across the wheel from the primary NOT used to make that secondary (i.e., green is a combination of blue and yellow, and sits directly opposite red on the wheel). These colors directly opposite on the wheel are called "complements" or complementary colors. Generally, the human eye is not attracted to equal amounts of complementary colors—neither seems to be the "main idea" and the eye wanders restlessly between them. However, complements can be used effectively together, if one is given a larger area of the design than the other. Think for a minute about the traditional "Christmas colors" of Western culture—in December, everywhere you look there is a combination of red, green, and white. Red and green are complementary colors, and most of the really attractive or successful combinations will have either red or green as the main color, using up about twice as much space as either of the other two. The white provides a value contrast and separates the complementary colors so the eye can appreciate them. When using complements, choose a "main color" which will cover about half the visual space. The complement to the main color should fill no more than ¼ of the visual space, and "less is more"—a little bit goes a long way. This is called the "accent color." The third color in the scheme (white, in the Christmas example above), is called the "contrast color." It takes up ¼ or a bit more of the visual space, and makes sure that the value contrast discussed above exists. Visual harmony is the result.

Warm or Cool

Another possible color scheme, less dramatic and generally more soft and soothing than use of complements, is to choose colors near each other on the wheel—either "warm" or "cool" colors. The colors on the same side of the wheel with red are the warm colors, and those on the same side of the wheel as blue are called cool colors. Think of the seasons: autumn or Indian summer, with its rich and warm array of browns, reds, oranges and yellows is a good example of a warm color palette. The winter landscape with blue sky, purple shadows, and evergreen trees is a cool palette example.

Have you ever noticed that some purples seem to "go" easily together, while some seem to be at war with each other? This has to do with the fact that purple is made of red and blue—a warm and a cool color combined. The quality of the purple (warm or cool) will depend on whether it contains more of the warm red or more of the cool blue in its mix. Any number of cool (predominantly blue) purples will look pleasing together, as will any number of warm (predominantly red) purples. But a reddish purple and a bluish purple together will create the same discomfort to the eye as the use of complementary colors next to each other.

Yellow is also a warm color and can be used to "warm up" colors from the cool side of the wheel. Greens, like purples, are an example of colors whose warmth or coolness is affected by the predominance of either the warm or cool primary in their makeup: think of the difference between warm grass or olive green (each with a large amount of yellow in their makeup), and sea green or forest green (each with a small amount of yellow in their makeup).

Safe and successful color choices can always be made by paying attention to the warmth or coolness of the choices. Use cool colors together freely, warm colors together freely; and remember that if you toss a color of the "other" quality into the mix, it will startle the eye. Many people find that they have a strong personal preference for either the warm or the cool colors. For others, it's a matter of mood or occasion, whether warm or cool is preferable. As an exercise in color awareness, look at your wardrobe, to determine the prevalence of warm and cool colors exhibited there.

Neutrals

In any color scheme the neutrals: black, white, gray, and beige can be used to provide unity, to tie together the whole visual experience, or to give relief (a slight separation of complementary or conflicting colors). Use neutrals freely, as they will always enhance the colors around them. A "scrap" project such as the traditional granny square blanket (a really random mix of lights and darks, warms and cools), is visually harmonious because of the neutral that surrounds each block of color.

Clear or Muted

The final color principle to keep in mind is the difference between "clear" and "muted" colors. When gray or beige is added to any color, that color is "muted" in either the cool (gray) or warm (beige) direction. These color differences can also be thought of as "bright" and "dull." Like warm and cool, the preference for clear or muted colors is highly personal. It's safe to use muted shades together, or to use clear shades together—but it gets a bit more tricky to mix the two types. When clear and muted colors are side by side, the whole project can take on a "muddy" appearance. It may seem complicated to decide whether a yarn color is muted or not; but if you find that two otherwise attractive colors just "don't go together," it's likely that one is muted and the other is clear.

(continued)

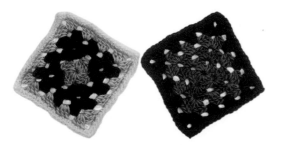

The square on left is an example of a cool color scheme. The square on right shows a warm color scheme.

Each bow comprises a clear and a muted shade of the same color. Placing clear and muted variants so close together makes each look less vibrant than if used with other colors of the same quality.

The Color Wheel (continued)

Choose one to keep in your scheme, and look for a substitute for the other. As an exercise, look back through the photos of the project samples in Chapters 1–5 to see if you can tell which are made in clear and which in muted color palettes. (Answers: Chain Gang Boa— version 1 in muted cool colors, optional variation with beads in warm muted colors; Bright and Bold Coasters—summer coasters in muted cool colors, winter wool coasters in clear cool colors; Roll Brim Cloche in warm muted colors, Phunky Phlowered Phone Carrier in clear warm brights; Longitude Scarf, both versions in muted warm and cool mixtures.)

Practice Swatch A— Basic Granny Square in One Color– 4 Rounds

With that quick lesson in color theory, you're ready to choose three colors (a light, a medium, and a dark) for your practice motif swatches!

Start with ch 4, and slip stitch to join in a ring.

Rnd 1: Ch 3 (counts as first dc), work 2 dc in ring, then make a corner increase by working ch 2, (3 dc in ring, ch 2) 3 times, join last ch with a sl st in top of beginning ch 3. At the end of the rnd, there are 4 groups of 3 dc, separated by ch-2 spaces.

TIP Be sure the sl st that finishes the round is made IN the top of the ch-3, not AROUND it. Inserting the hook under the chain and working around it will create an extra space in the stitching, which will seriously affect the finished appearance of the piece, and may also lead to difficulties in determining where stitches should be placed in the following round.

Completed Rnd 1, correctly joined.

Rnd 2: Ch 4 (counts as dc and ch-1), place marker in 3rd ch of the ch-4, skip next group of dc, (3 dc, ch 2, 3 dc) in next ch-2 space. This sequence in parentheses will be repeated at every corner throughout the granny square, no matter how many rounds are made.

Round 2, started and first corner worked.

The corner increase to keep the square flat and correctly shaped is made by working this sequence in each of the four corners of each round. Many patterns, having thus explained the corner increase one time, will, in following rounds, simply say, "Make corner." This is especially true in older patterns.

*Ch 1, skip next 3-dc group, work corner increase (that is, 3 dc, ch 2, 3 dc) in next ch-2 space; repeat from * one time, ch 1, skip next 3-dc group, (3 dc, ch 2, 2 dc) in last ch-2 space, sl st to join in marked 3rd ch of beginning ch-4. Again, be sure to work into and not around the chain.

Rnd 3: Sl st into ch-1 space, ch 3, 2 dc in same ch-1 space.

(continued)

Troubleshooting—Common Granny Square Mistakes

When a granny square "goes wrong," it's usually because of one or more of the following common mistakes. In each case, the work needs to be ripped out to the point where the mistake occurred. Because of the way each round builds on the previous one, it doesn't work to try to adjust the number of stitches in an outer round, if the inner ones are "off."

Mistake #1—If the first round contains 3 or 5 groups of 3 dc, the resulting shape will not be a square, and the increases won't be correct for keeping it flat. Swatch on left shows result of 5 dc groups in Rnd 1; swatch on right shows result of 3 dc groups in Rnd 1.

Mistake #2—If the joining sl st at the ends of rounds is worked around instead of into the chain, a hole results, and in a following round, it's then easy to interpret that hole as a ch-1 or ch-2 space needing to be worked in. This results in too many 3-dc groups on the side where rounds begin and end. Markers show slip stitches worked around the beginning chain.

Mistake #3—This square lost a corner, at the marked spot, because there's only one 3-dc group in the corner space, instead of the proper corner increase.

Practice Swatch A (continued)

*Ch 1, (3 dc, ch 2, 3 dc) in next ch-2 space, ch 1, 3 dc in next ch-1 space, repeat from * twice more (3 corners formed), ch 1, (3 dc, ch 2, 3 dc) in last ch-2 space, ch 1, sl st to join in top of beginning ch-3.

Rnd 4: Ch 4, place marker in 3rd ch made, 3 dc in next ch-1 space, ch 1, work corner in next ch-2 space, *ch 1, 3 dc in next ch-1 space*; repeat between * and * to next corner ch-2 spaced, work corner in ch-2 space; repeat between * and * to next corner, repeat entire sequence of side and corner around, ending with 2 dc in last ch-1 space, sl st to join in marked 3rd ch of beginning ch-4. Fasten off.

Optional Edging Round: Attach a second color, with a sc in any ch-1 (side) space. Work 1 sc in each dc and 1 sc in each ch-space to next corner. Work (2 sc, ch 1, 2 sc) in corner. Repeat sides and corners around, ending with a sl st to join last st to first stitch. Fasten off.

TIP Locating the top of the first stitch in a 3-dc group— Remember that the top of any crochet stitch is slightly offset from its vertical stem or post. When alternating between working in a space and working in the first stitch after the space, look for the V at the top and slightly to the right of the first stitch in the next group.

Sometimes it's a little difficult to locate the top of the first stitch after a space!

Practice Swatch B— Traditional Three-Color Granny Square

Call your lightest chosen color A; the medium color B, and the darkest color C.

With A, work foundation chain and ring, the same as in Swatch #1.

Rnd 1: Work as in first square (page 66). At end of Rnd 1, fasten off A.

Rnd 2: Attach B with a dc in any corner ch-2 space.

TIP Attaching a new yarn with a dc—Place a slip knot of the new color on the hook. Yo before inserting hook into indicated stitch or space. Insert the hook and complete the stitch as usual. This method minimizes the number of places in a piece that a ch-3 has to stand for a dc—since that's functional, but never looks quite right. This method is also invisible, no slip stitch to show where the new yarn was attached!

Complete that corner, ch 1, *skip next 3-dc group, work corner, ch 1; repeat from * around, ending with sl st in first dc.

Rnd 3: Ch 4 (counts as dc and ch 1), mark 3rd ch made, skip to next corner ch-2 space, work corner, ch 1, *3 dc in next ch-1 space, ch 1, corner in ch-2 corner space; repeat from * until all 4 corners are worked, 2 dc in last ch-1 space, join with a sl st to marked ch of beginning ch 3. Fasten off B.

Rnd 4: Attach C with a dc in any ch-2 corner space (counts as first dc of corner). Complete the corner, ch 1, work around in pattern, working (3 dc, ch 1) in each ch-1 space on the sides of the square, and (3 dc, ch 2, 3 dc) in each corner ch-2 space, end with ch 1, sl st to join to first dc of round. Fasten off C. Weave in all yarn ends, into matching color yarn.

Optional edging round: A sc edging around each granny can make joining several squares easier and more attractive. It's also an effective tool in the color scheme. Try using A again to edge the completed square, as in Practice Square #1.

Now that both single-color and multi-color granny squares are familiar, they can be made in different sizes, and combined into a variety of projects!

Troubleshooting—The Logic of Granny Squares

Some people find granny squares confusing because of the alternating nature of the stitch pattern's repetitions. If you're simply following one instruction after another, it's hard to understand why sometimes the round starts with ch 3, counting as the first stitch of the round, but sometimes starts with ch 4, which will stand as the last stitch of the round! If only following a series of separate instructions, it's difficult to see why sometimes there's a ch-1 space, and sometimes there's a ch-2 space! But if the "big picture" is kept in view, it all becomes clear. The granny square is really an exercise in logic, a series of "if-then" statements:

IF the round begins with a space immediately to the left of the sl st join,

THEN ch 3 and work in that space; it's the next possible place to make a 3-dc group.

IF the round begins with a space immediately to the right of the sl st join,

THEN, ch 4, and skip to the next place where a 3-dc group can be worked. Work always progresses around the square moving to the left.

IF the space being worked is on the side of the square,

THEN it's a ch-1 space. All three stitches of the dc group will fit in that space. More chains on a straight side would create "ruffles" as we saw earlier in learning to increase keeping a shape flat.

IF the space being worked is on a corner of the square,

THEN it's a ch-2 space. Since two whole 3-dc groups will have to be worked into that space, it needs to be wider than a "side" space, to accommodate the greater number of stitches. It also takes more chains to work around the corner (increasing) than to work along a straight side.

PROJECT 6:
Grab-and-Go Granny Bag

Whether used for books, groceries, or skeins of yarn, this versatile and spacious bag is a great accessory! The bag is made from two sizes of granny squares and a larger square that's a solid stitch variation on the granny square theme. The sample is shown in a warm and muted color scheme, but the project would look equally great in cool, clear jewel tones, or neon brights. Or feel free to use your imagination and what you've learned about confident color choices!

WHAT YOU'LL LEARN

- How to connect individual motifs by three different methods

- How to make a solid stitch motif, a variation on the granny square theme

WHAT YOU'LL NEED

YARN

- 1 skein each of 5 colors (A, light, 300 yds [276 m]; B and D medium solids 100 yds [92 m]; C dark solid 100 yds [92 m]; F, variegated or space-dyed in a related color 200 yds [184 m])

- Shown: Caron's Simply Soft (100% Acrylic; 6 oz./315 yds), 0008 Autumn Maize (A), 0009 Garnet (B), 0013 Nutmeg (C), 0010 Cypress (D), and Caron's Simply Soft Paints (100% Acrylic; 4 oz/200 yds), 0008 Sunset (E)

HOOK

- Size H (5 mm) or size needed to obtain gauge

NOTIONS

- One stitch marker
- Large-eyed yarn needle

GAUGE

- Completed Round 1 of each motif measures 1½" to 1¾" (3.8 to 4.5 cm) from side to side. However, exact gauge is not essential for this project

FINISHED SIZE

- 12½" (32 cm) square; strap is 3½" wide by 40" (9 × 103 cm) long

STITCHES AND ABBREVIATIONS USED

- chain = ch
- slip stitch = sl st
- single crochet = sc
- double crochet = dc
- stitch(es) = st(s)
- round = rnd
- single crochet 2 together (decrease) = sc2tog (see instructions in Project 4)
- special stitch = corner (3 dc, ch 2, 3 dc)

INSTRUCTIONS

Notes

1. Stitch counts for rounds appear in {brackets} following round instructions.

2. All rounds of each square are worked with right side facing.

First Side of Bag

1 Make 4 medium granny squares following instructions below. Each square begins with A at center. Rnds 2–4 are worked with one of the contrast colors: B, C, D, and E. Final round is worked with A.

With A, ch 4, sl st to join in a ring.

Rnd 1: Ch 3, 2 dc in ring, ch 2, *3 dc in ring, ch 2; repeat from * twice more, join last ch in top of beginning ch-3 with a sl st. Fasten off A. {Four 3-dc groups, 4 ch-2 corner spaces}

Rnd 2: Attach contrast color with a dc in any corner ch-2 space, (2 dc, ch 2, 3 dc) in same space, ch 1, *skip next 3 dc, work corner in next ch-2 space (see special stitch, above), ch 1; repeat from * around, ending with sl st to join last ch to first dc of rnd. {Eight 3-dc groups, 4 ch-1 spaces on sides of square, 4 ch-2 spaces at corners}

Rnd 3: Ch 4, mark 3rd ch made, skip next 3-dc group, *work corner in next ch-2 space, ch 1, skip 3 dc, 3 dc in next ch-1 space, ch 1; repeat from * around, 2 dc in last ch-1 space, sl st to join in marked 3rd ch of beginning ch-4. {Twelve 3-dc groups, 4 ch-2 spaces at corners, 8 ch-1 spaces along sides}

Rnd 4: Sl st into ch-1 space immediately to the left of join just made, ch 3, 2 dc in same ch-1 space, ch 1, skip to next ch-2 space, *work corner in ch-2 space, ch 1, 3 dc in next ch-1 space, ch 1, 3 dc in next ch-1 space, ch 1; repeat from * around, ending with ch 1, sl st to join last ch in top of beginning ch-3. Fasten off. {Sixteen 3-dc groups, 4 ch-2 spaces at corners, and 12 ch-1 spaces along sides}.

Rnd 5: Attach A with a dc in any corner ch-2 space, (dc, ch 2, 2 dc) in same ch-2 space, *dc in each st and in each ch-1 space to next corner, work (2 dc, ch 2, 2 dc) in corner ch-2 space. {19 dc along each side, and 4 ch-2 spaces at corners}. Note that the corners are slightly different on this round of solid stitching! Fasten off and weave in all yarn tails.

2 Join four granny squares with a whip stitch seam. Hold two squares with wrong sides together, so that right side of work faces outward on both sides.

Thread about an arm's length of A onto large-eyed yarn needle. Leaving at least 8" (20.5 cm) of tail, insert the needle under one arm of the V at the top of the first stitch of the first square, AND under one arm of the V at the top of the first stitch of the second square. The seam will look neatest if needle is inserted under the "inner" strands, the two touching each other as the squares are held together. Pull the yarn through, making sure to leave tail still hanging. Holding the two squares together so that corners and spaces match, match the stitches from the two squares and continue with the next pair of stitches: insert needle from the same side as the first whip-stitch, pull through, insert from same direction in next pair of stitches, all the way across the row. All stitches are made with the needle pointed in the same direction, although which direction that is will depend on what's comfortable for each stitcher. Some prefer to push the needle toward themselves; while some prefer to push the needle away. As long as all stitches in the row are consistent, the result will be the same.

When the first two squares are joined, fasten off yarn and weave in the beginning and ending tail of the seam. Repeat the process for the second pair of squares, again making sure that the right side of the work faces outward, so that you're looking at the same side of the square as while crocheting it. Now hold the two rectangles in the same manner and sew a longer seam, starting with nearly two arms' length of yarn to ensure that it's enough for weaving in tails. When all four squares are joined, work edging.

3 Edging for First Side

Rnd 1: Attach D with a sc in any ch-2 space, with right side of work facing, work 2 more sc in same ch-2 space, *sc in every st along side to next ch-2 space, working 1 sc in each ch-1 space and 1 sc in end of seam, 3 sc in next ch-2 space; repeat from * around, joining final st to first st with a sl st. {41 sc along each side and 3 sc in each corner}. Weave in all remaining yarn tails and set first side of bag aside.

Second Side of Bag

4 Make one large motif as follows:

With A, ch 4, sl st to join in ring.

Rnd 1: Work as Rnd 1 for medium granny square above, but DO NOT fasten off at completion of rnd. {Four 3-dc groups}

Rnd 2: Ch 3, dc in each of next 2 sts, *(2 dc, ch 2, 2 dc) corner in next ch-2 space (notice that this is a slightly different corner from that used in the granny squares), dc in each of next 3 sts; repeat from * around, ending with (2 dc, ch 2, 2 dc) in last ch-2 space, join last st to top of beginning ch-3 with a sl st. Fasten off A, leaving long enough tail to weave in securely. {7 dc on each side of square}

Rnd 3: Attach B with a dc in first st to the left of any corner ch-2 space. *dc in each st to next ch-2 space, (2 dc, ch 2, 2 dc) in ch-2 space; repeat from * around, ending with sl st to join last st of last corner with first st of rnd. {11 dc on each side of square}

Rnd 4: Ch 3, *dc in each st to next ch-2 space, work corner in ch-2 space; repeat from * around, ending with dc in each of last 2 sts; sl st to join. Fasten off B. {15 dc per side of square}

Rnd 5: Attach C with a dc in first dc to the left of any ch-2 space. Work same as Rnd 3. {19 dc per side of square}

Rnd 6: Work same as Rnd 4. At end of rnd, fasten off C. {23 dc per side}

Rnd 7: With E (instead of B), work same as Rnd 3. {27 dc per side}

Rnd 8: Work same as Rnd 4. Fasten off E. {31 dc per side}

Rnd 9: With A, work same as Rnd 3. {35 dc per side}

Rnd 10: Work same as Rnd 4. Fasten off A. {39 dc per side}

Rnd 11: With D, work same as Rnd 3. Fasten off D. {43 dc per side}.

(continued)

Weave in all yarn tails securely into matching color yarn areas. If stitch counts are correct, the stitches of the edge of this motif will match the edging stitches of completed first side of bag. (The corner sc of the first side "matches" the ch-2 space of the second side). Set completed second side of bag aside.

Strap

5 Make 12 small motifs following instructions below.

Beginning, Rnds 1 and 2: With E, follow directions for Rnds 1 and 2 of large motif. Fasten off. {7 dc per side}

Rnd 3: Attach A with a sc in first st to left of any ch-2 space, *sc in each st to next ch-2 space, 4 sc in ch-2 space; repeat from * around, ending with a sl st to join last sc to first sc of rnd. Fasten off. Weave in tails.

6 Assemble Strap

Hold 2 small squares with wrong sides together and edge stitches aligned. Working through all 4 loops (both loops of edge stitches of each square) attach A at right hand edge and work 11 sl sts across.

Repeat sl st seam till all 12 motifs are joined, end to end, in a long line. When complete, weave in all yarn tails securely.

7 Strap Edging

Attach D with a sc in st at right hand edge of either short end of strap, *sc in each st across to corner, ch 1, rotate to work along long side of strap, sc in each st of long side, also working 1 sc in end of each seam, ch 1, rotate and repeat from * one more time. Join last stitch to first with a sl st. Fasten off D and weave in tails.

Assemble Bag

8 Crochet Bag Front and Back Together

Hold first and second sides of bag together, with wrong sides together and right sides facing outward. Attach D with a sc through both loops of both pieces at any corner, *sc in each st across, matching sts of both sides, and working through both loops of each side (inserting hook under 4 loops to begin each st) to next corner, 3 sc in corner; repeat from * 2 more times until 3 sides of the bag are crocheted together, on 4th, open, side, work through only 1 thickness (inserting hook under only 2 loops of one side of bag for each st), sc in each st across one side of bag, turn bag and work 1 sc in each st across other side of bag, join final sc to first sc of rnd with a sl st, ch 1 and continue in same direction, working another rnd of sc across open top of bag, join with a sl st. Fasten off.

9 Attach Strap to Bag

Position one short end of stap inside top edge of bag with wrong sides together, so that the 12 sts of strap match last 12 sts of bag top edging. With D, sl st through both pieces, matching sts, across. Fasten off. Repeat with opposite end of strap and opposite side of bag.

TIP Slip Stitch Seam—Working a series of slip stitches is another way to join motifs or other pieces of crocheted fabric together. As with any other slip stitch, insert the hook through the indicated loops or stitches, draw up a loop to the front and immediately through the loop on the hook. Make sure to pull the loop through far enough that the resulting stitch is not too tight. Extra tight slip stitch seams will cause puckering of the work. The seam should appear on the right side of the work as a flat triple-braid.

With D, work one more rnd of sc edging across bag's top edge and long side of strap. At inner corner where strap intersects with bag, sc2tog over 1 st of strap and 1 st of bag. Join final st to first st with a sl st. Repeat with opposite side of strap and opposite side of bag. Fasten off. Weave in any remaining yarn tails securely.

TIP The Right Seam for the Job—In this project we've used three different seaming methods. Other methods also exist, and some of them will be covered later. Generally, a stitcher may choose his or her favorite method, and many patterns will merely direct, "seam pieces together." The seam methods for this project were chosen because of their differing characteristics for different structural functions. The whip stitch that joined the four grannies of the first side, is a nearly invisible seam when sewn carefully, matching stitches. However, the seam is only one strand thick, and so is not as sturdy as some others. It was chosen because this area of the bag is not in much danger of stretching or being otherwise stressed, and the invisible nature of the seam means that the eye's attention is on the colors of the granny squares, rather than on the seam. The slip stitch seams of the strap were chosen because a strap needs to be both flat and very sturdy. A slip stitch seam is NOT invisible, but is rather decorative, and the motifs being joined were fairly plain. The slip stitch seam is also very strong, and also doesn't cause a ridge, which might irritate a shoulder if the bag is full and heavy! The single crochet seam of the bag's outer edges was chosen because it creates both a decorative ridged edging, and puts the largest number of strands of yarn in the place where the seam will receive the most structural stress. So, when working other projects, and choosing your own seaming method, keep in mind the function and appearance of the seamed area, and choose the best seam for the job!

Bonus Project Idea— Patchwork Blanket

Make 13 large motifs and 12 squares composed of 4 medium granny squares each (just like the two sides of the bag). Place large squares at the 4 corners and arrange the completed squares so there are 5 squares in each of 5 rows, alternating large motifs and the 4-granny squares. Slip stitch to make a sturdy and flat join, or sc together for a decorative raised ridge. The blanket can either be edged with rounds of sc, or with strips of small granny squares, such as used in the bag's handle. When edging, remember to increase in each corner, by working 3 sc in the corner stitch or 4 sc in a ch-2 space at a corner.

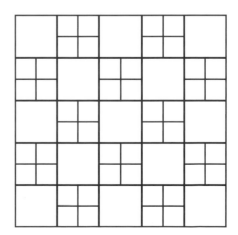

Putting It All Together

The lessons learned in this section will build on your basic skills and give you confidence as you choose projects to crochet. You will be introduced to the international stitch symbols for crochet and learn how to interpret them to follow instructions. Your crochet horizons will be expanded as you learn more basic stitches and discover interesting stitch patterns and textures that develop from using combinations of stitches over several rows.

CHAPTER 7:
Combining Stitches, Reading Charts

Crochet is truly an international art, with deep cultural roots in many areas of both Asia and Europe. Today, designers from Brazil, Russia, Ukraine, Japan, Korea, Western Europe, and North America can all communicate patterns and instructions by using a set of international stitch symbols.

It might be intimidating to take on the entire array of symbols, especially since the stitches they represent haven't been taught yet! However a full chart of the stitch diagram symbols does appear on page 187. Let's start with the stitches we've learned. You already know what the actual stitch looks like in your work, and you know their names and the abbreviations that describe them in a pattern. It's only one more step to recognize the graphic symbol for each:

⬭ = chain (ch)

• = slip stitch (sl st)

✛ = single crochet (sc)

⋀ = single crochet decrease (sc2tog)

╤ = double crochet (dc)

// = fasten off yarn

⇄ = directional arrows

WHAT YOU'LL LEARN.............

- How to read a simple stitch diagram in rows
- How to create a swatch from a stitch symbol diagram

WHAT YOU'LL NEED ....

YARN

- About 10 yds (9.15 m) of scrap yarn, worsted weight

HOOK

- Size H (5 mm)

Practice Swatch #1

When we read written English, we read from left to right, but this is not necessarily the direction of movement in reading a symbol diagram. In diagrams, what matters is the direction of the stitching. When working in rows, we turn the work so that every row is worked from right to left, but if the right side of the fabric is facing, then one row is stitches whose top-V's face left, and the next is a row whose top-V's face to the right, back and forth from row to row. This is the way stitch diagrams are read when the work is in rows.

Follow the diagram, as explained in the caption, and make the swatch. If you find yourself "stuck," here is the written pattern in familiar abbreviated English form:

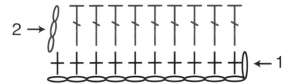

Read the diagram starting at the bottom left. The chains progress across the bottom. The last chain is at an angle, showing that its function is the "turning chain." Row 1 is read from right to left. The number "1" is at the side where the eye should start reading. Row 2, read from left to right, has its beginning chain at its start, and the number "2" stands at the beginning of the row. The diagram is read by understanding that each symbol is a little picture of an individual stitch.

Foundation: Ch 11, turn.

Row 1: Sc in 2nd ch from hook and each ch across. Turn. {10 sc}

Row 2: Ch 3, dc in 2nd stitch and each st across. Fasten off.

Here's the finished swatch:

- How to read a symbol diagram for crochet in rounds
- How to create a small motif from a symbol diagram

YARN

- About 10 yds (9.15 m) of scrap yarn, worsted weight

HOOK

- Size H (5 mm)

Practice Swatch #2, Rounds

When working in rounds, the diagram is read from where the crochet begins: the center, moving outward, just as the crochet rounds progress outward from the center.

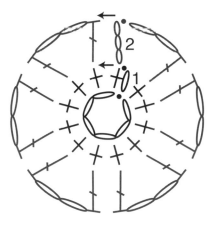

Start reading at the center, counting the chain symbols. The slip stitch symbol notes where the next round will begin. The next round is printed in a different color in this and many other diagrams.

(continued)

Practice Swatch #2 (continued)

The symbols for the stitches of Round 1 don't line up exactly over the chain symbols, because as in most motifs, the single crochets are being worked into the ring, and there are more stitches in Round 1 than in the foundation ring. Count the symbols for sc to see how many stitches to work. Most motifs are worked with right side facing, as were our motifs in Chapter 6. If a circle diagram wants you to turn the work and work in the opposite direction, a little arrow will direct you at the beginning of a round. In this case, the direction doesn't change, so proceed with right side of Round 1 still facing, working in the same direction. Round 2 begins with chains, and then each dc symbol is standing directly on top of the stitch into which it should be worked. Here's the written pattern, in case you need to refer to it—but you'll gain diagram skill most quickly by trying to "see" the stitches in the diagram first and only referring to the written words when really necessary.

Foundation: Ch 6, join with sl st to form ring.

Rnd 1: Ch 1, work 12 sc in ring; join last st to first with a sl st.

Rnd 2: Ch 3, dc in next st, ch 2, *dc in each of next 2 sts, ch 2; repeat from * around, ending with sl st in top of beginning ch-3. Fasten off. {12 dc and 6 ch-2 spaces}

Here's the resulting swatch:

WHAT YOU'LL LEARN . . . .

- More practice in following a multi-round diagram
- How to make the familiar granny square without written directions

WHAT YOU'LL NEED . . . .

YARN

- Approximately 25 yds (23 m) scrap worsted yarn in each of two colors, A and B

HOOK

- Size H (5 mm)

Practice Swatch #3

Here's a stitch symbol diagram version of the pattern for the 3-color granny square made as a practice swatch in Chapter 6. Try following the diagram without looking back at the written directions. Color changes are shown by the use of different colored ink in the diagram. When finished, the square should be the same as the one already made.

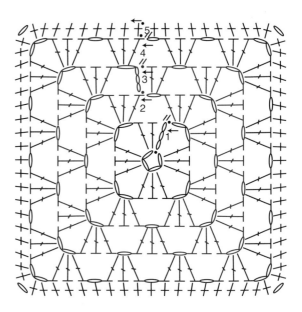

PROJECT 7:
Flower Power Retro Beanie

Now that some of the mystery of symbol diagrams has been removed, it's time to make a whole project by following these international symbols. Many crocheters find that this becomes their preferred pattern type. Others always lean toward written word/abbreviation directions, but both groups benefit from being able to refer to the "other" set of directions when in doubt as to meaning in the pattern being followed.

The Flower Power Hat will give you opportunity to practice following stitch symbol diagrams, while also offering the word directions. In the remaining chapters, symbol diagrams will be provided for pattern stitches, as part of the patterns' instructions. For now, it's probably best to start this project with the smaller flowers, made from simpler diagrams, and then make the motifs, following the more complex diagram. The motifs in this project are similar to granny squares (groups of stitches are created in chain spaces rather than in stitch tops), but are an example of another popular type of motif—the circle-to-square. Rounds 1 and 2 create a circle with eight sections. Rounds 3 and 4 use placement of the increases and height of stitches to create four corners and our straight sides—a square! The single crochets of Round 5 provide a stable edge to use in joining squares together.

WHAT YOU'LL LEARN . . . .

- How to make an entire project by following symbol diagrams, with written directions as supplementary reference
- How to make a circle-to-square motif, useful for additional projects, such as blankets, scarves, and so on
- How to construct a hat from 5 flat squares
- How to wet block a wool or wool blend project

WHAT YOU'LL NEED . . . .

YARN

- 1 ball each of 3 colors of light worsted weight yarn
- Shown: "Sheep(ish)" by Vickie Howell for Caron (70% Acrylic, 30% Wool; 3 oz/167 yds), 0017 Turquoise(ish) (A), 0007 Hot Pink(ish) (B), and 0012 Yellow(ish) (C)

HOOK

- Size G (4.25 mm) or hook to obtain gauge

NOTIONS

- Large-eyed yarn needle
- One stitch marker

(continued)

WHAT YOU'LL NEED . . . .

FINISHED SIZE

- Teen/Adult
- Finished circumference (unstretched) at edge = 21" (53.5 cm)
- Height from edge to crown = 9" (23 cm)

GAUGE

- Diameter of completed small flower (Rnds 1–3) = 2½" (6.5 cm). Width of completed motif measured edge to edge = 5 to 5¼" (12.5 to 13.5 cm). Correct gauge is important for finished fit of hat.

STITCHES AND ABBREVIATIONS USED

- chain = ch
- slip stitch = sl st
- single crochet = sc
- double crochet = dc
- stitch(es) = st(s)
- space(s) = sp(s) usually designated by number of chain used to create (i.e. ch-2 sp = space made by 2 ch).
- round = rnd
- place marker = pm

INSTRUCTIONS

Notes

1. Stitch counts appear in {brackets} following instructions for rounds.

2. Remember when attaching new yarn colors, to leave sufficient tails for weaving in. It is acceptable to crochet over a starting or finishing tail, but this is only the first stage of the weaving in, and the tail must be long enough to thread onto needle for secure finishing.

3. In this pattern, since chains are worked AROUND and not INTO, it's best to chain rather tightly.

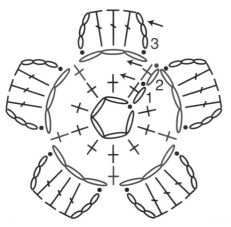

Two colors of ink make the rounds easily visible, but the flower is worked in one color of yarn, without fastening off until completed.

1 Make Two Small Flowers

Make one with B and one with C, leaving 10" (25.5 cm) tails at start and finish, for sewing flower to hat. Follow the stitch diagram. Written instructions follow.

Ch 5 and sl st to join in ring {5-ch ring}

Rnd 1: Ch 1, work 10 sc in ring, sl st to join last st to first st.

Rnd 2: Ch 1, sc in same st as join, *ch 3, skip next sc, sc in next sc; repeat from * around, joining last ch-3 to first sc with a sl st. {5 ch-3 sps}

Rnd 3: *Sl st in next ch-3 sp, ch 3, 3 dc in same sp, ch 3, sl st in same sp.

(continued)

Repeat from * in each ch-3 sp around. Fasten off. {5 petals, each consisting of sl st, ch 3, 3 dc, ch 3, sl st}

2 Make One Large, Two-Color Flower

Leave 10" (25.5 cm) beginning and ending yarn tails, for sewing flower to hat.

With C, ch 6, sl st to join in ring. {6-ch ring}

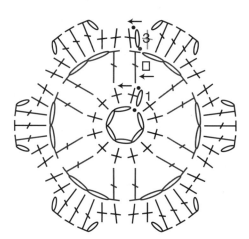

Foundation ring and Rnd 1 are shown in first color; Rnds 2 and 3 are shown in second color. Note the // symbol where first yarn is fastened off.

Rnd 1: Ch 1, work 12 sc in ring, sl st to join last st to first st. Fasten off C. {12 sc in ring}

Rnd 2: Attach A with a dc in any stitch, dc in next st, ch 2, *dc in each of next 2 sts, ch 2; repeat from * around, sl st to join last ch to first dc. {6 ch-2 sps, 12 dc}

If the Rnd 1 join is done in the turning chain, instead of the top of the first stitch, it will seem like 13 stitches in Round 1 when Round 2 is worked. Be careful to always join the last stitch to the top of the first stitch, to keep the correct number of stitches in each round. Correctly finished Rnd 2 consists of 12 dc and 6 ch-2 spaces.

Rnd 3: Ch 1, * sc in each of next 2 dc, (sc, ch 1, 3 dc, ch 1, sc) in next ch-2 sp; repeat from * around, joining final sc to first sc. Fasten off, leaving long tail for sewing flower to hat. {6 petals}

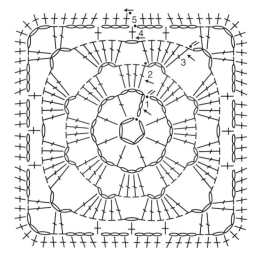

Ink colors in the diagram correspond to yarn colors A, B, and C. Note // symbol when yarn is to be fastened off.

3 Make Five Circle-to-Square Motifs

With A, ch 5, sl st to join in ring.

Rnd 1: Ch 6, PM in 3rd ch made (counts as dc and ch-3), *dc in ring, ch 3; repeat from * 6 more times, join last ch to marked ch with a sl st. Fasten off A. {8 ch-3 sps, 8 dc}

Rnd 2: Attach B with a dc in any ch-3 sp, work 3 more dc in same sp, ch 3, *in next sp work 4 dc, ch 3; repeat from * around, ending with a sl st in first dc to join. Fasten off B. {Eight 4-dc groups, 8 ch-3 sps)

Rnd 3: (Note: This round is where the circle begins to change into a square, through varying the length of chain between dc groups. The four evenly spaced longer chains will become the corners of the square, in Rnd 4.) Attach C with a dc in any ch-3 sp, work 5 more dc in same sp, ch 1, *6 dc in next sp, ch 3, in 6 dc in next sp, ch 1; repeat from * 2 more times, 6 dc in last sp, ch 3 (for corner), sl st to join last ch to first dc of round. Fasten off C. {Eight 6-dc groups, 4 ch-1sps, 4 ch-3 sps}

Rnd 4: (Note: In Rnd 4 the "squaring process" is completed, through use of taller and shorter stitches, and corner increases.) Attach A with a sc in any ch-1 sp, ch 3, sc BETWEEN 3rd and 4th sts of next 6-dc group (see photo).

To work between stitches, ignore the Vs at the top, and insert the hook from front to back, between the vertical posts of the two indicated stitches.

TIP "Any Stitch" Yarn Attachments—Although it's common for symbol diagrams to show the starts of all rounds aligned with each other, when the written directions state that a join may be made in "any stitch," it will actually be easier to do the weaving in of tails if the rounds begin at different places, rather than the straight alignment shown in the diagram. Attach the new yarn in any indicated stitch, and then follow the diagram from the beginning of that round, even though your round is oriented differently. The progressive photographs for this motif will demonstrate staggered color attachments; look closely for the slip stitches that mark the ends of previous rounds, in relation to the new round's point of attachment.

Don't be concerned by the "ruffly" appearance of completed Rounds 2 and 3. The "excess" chain increases will be taken up in Round 4!

Ch 3, (2 dc, ch 3, 2 dc) in corner ch-3 sp, ch 3, sc between 3rd and 4th sts of next 6-dc group, ch 3, *sc in next ch-1 sp, ch 3, sc between 3rd and 4th sts of next 6-dc group, ch 3, (2 dc, ch 3, 2 dc) in corner ch-3 sp, ch 3, sc between 3rd and 4th sts of next 6-dc group, ch 3; repeat from * 2 more times, sl st to join last ch to first sc. DO NOT FASTEN OFF. {20 ch-3 sps, 4 corners worked in taller sts}.

Rnd 5: Ch 1, 3 sc in each of next 2 ch-3 sps, at corner sc in each of next 2 dc, 5 sc in ch-3 sp, sc in each of next 2 dc, *3 sc in each of next 4 ch-3 sps, sc in each of next 2 dc, 5 sc in ch-3 sp, sc in each of next 2 dc; repeat from * 2 more times, sl st to join last sc to first sc. Fasten off. Weave in all yarn tails securely as each motif is completed.

(continued)

TIP Why Such a Small Hook/Tight Gauge?—In previous projects, we've used a H-K (5-6.5 mm hook with worsted weight yarn. This project calls for a much tighter construction, with a smaller hook for the same size of yarn. Why? Because a smaller hook, in relation to the size of yarn, creates a stiffer, more structured fabric. These motifs are very open and lacy in their pattern. In order for the hat to hold its shape, the motifs need to be slightly stiff; hence the tight gauge and smaller hook. If the same motifs were being made for a blanket or garment, they would be softer and drape well if worked with a larger hook, and a finished size of about 5½" to 6" (14 to 15 cm) across. In Chapter 8, we'll address other aspects of crochet that affect the softness or drape of the fabrics being created.

4 Assemble Hat

Beginning at the center sc of a 5-sc corner, hold center motif with one side motif, wrong sides together. Matching sts of one side, sc through both thicknesses across. {22 sc}. Fasten off. Repeat with center motif and each side motif, until pieces are assembled as in layout photo above. Next, crochet 4 side seams in same manner, one at a time, from crown to outside edge. {22 sc per seam}. Fasten off and weave in ends, on inside of hat.

5 Finish Hat with Edging and Flowers

Edging

Rnd 1: With right side of hat facing, attach A with a sc at center of edge of any square. (This is now the back of the hat), sc in each st and in each seam end, around, join with a sl st. Fasten off.

Rnd 2: With right side of hat facing, attach C with a sc in first sc of Rnd 1, sc in each st around, join with a sl st. Fasten off.

Rnd 3: With B, repeat Rnd 2.

Rnd 4: With A, repeat Rnd 2.

Weave in all yarn tails, on inside of hat.

Sew Flowers to Hat

With right side of hat facing, locate center back (where edging rounds began and ended). Move to the right 1½ motifs, to side seam. Use yarn tails of large flower to sew flower, centered on seam, with edges of lower petals just past Rnd 4 of edging. Position small flower in C just to right of, and touching large flower, with center of small flower centered below center of hat motif. Sew in place, using flower's yarn tails. Position small flower in B,

Make sure that the right side of each motif is facing up in the layout. This will make it easy to be certain to crochet them together correctly.

just above, and touching, large flower, centered on side seam of hat. Alternatively, flowers may be positioned anywhere on hat, as desired. Sew into place, using flower's yarn tails. Weave in any remaining yarn tails.

Blocking

When a natural fiber is a significant (25% or more) part of the makeup of the yarn, the option exists for blocking the finished project. In Chapter 2 we discussed steaming and felting as blocking methods, but wet blocking is usually best for non-felted projects with wool and wool blends. Wet blocking will help the wool soften, and will relax the stitches into a natural relationship with one another, creating a "finished" look to the fabric and the project. If any yarn tails are not as securely woven in as you had thought, blocking will help them to "pop out" visibly, so they can be threaded in where they're hidden on the wrong side of the fabric.

Begin by soaking the hat in cool water with a little of one of the following: delicate washing product such as Woolite, white vinegar, or a non-rinse product such as Soak or Eucalan. Allow the hat to soak submerged in cool water for 15 to 30 minutes. Pour off the water, and squeeze excess water out of the hat, being careful NOT to twist or wring. If using Woolite or another product requiring rinse, soak a second time, for 5 minutes or so, in clear water and squeeze the clear water through the hat before pouring off. Roll the hat in a dry towel and squeeze the roll to remove most of the water. Gently lay the hat out on another dry towel, and use fingers to shape edge, petals of flowers, and so on. so that there are no areas with curling or crookedness. Allow hat to dry, out of direct sun. When dry, the hat is ready to wear, and should be softer and smoother in appearance than if unblocked.

Yarns made entirely from synthetic fibers, such as acrylic and nylon, are less responsive to usual blocking methods, but may respond well to being washed gently and then tumbled at low heat in a dryer, if the yarn label permits tumble drying. Synthetic fibers soften and become pliable when heated (instead of felting together, as wool does). They firm into a permanent shape as they cool, which is why "permanent press" cycles on dryers have a gradual cooling of the temperature, so that the wrinkles removed from fabric by the heat and tumbling motion are not re-set into the fabric by the tumbling action stopping while fiber is still warm and soft.

Yarns made from delicate fibers, such as silk or alpaca, require the gentlest blocking of all: spritz blocking. In this method, the finished item is laid out flat and dry on a towel. Cool water is then spritzed on, dampening the surface thoroughly. While damp, the item is finger-pressed into shape, and then allowed to dry.

Fiber blends in yarns present some challenge in choosing a blocking method, but in general, it's good to start at the gentlest method (less heat, moisture, friction, and pulling stress). If gentle blocking gives the desired finish, great! If an edge or corner still wants to curl, or a seam still looks bunchy or won't lie flat, then it's time to try a slightly more aggressive blocking method.

Bonus Ideas for Flowers and Circle-to-Square Motifs

- Make one or more flowers in yarn matching or coordinating with the Roll-Brim Cloche made as Project 3, and embellish the hat for another fun and stylish look.
- Attach a pin-back jewelry finding, or a hair barrette, to a flower for a quick accessory.
- Make ten Circle-to-Square Motifs, and either slip stitch or whip stitch them together in a long line, as with the strap in Project 6. Edge with rounds of sc, as in the Flower Power Hat, and use flowers to decorate one or both of the scarf ends, instead of fringe!
- Sixty-four motifs, worked with an H or I (5.00 or 5.50mm) hook and joined by any seaming method in 8 rows of 8 motifs, then edged as in the Flower Power Hat, would make a bright and cheery throw blanket, with or without flowers to embellish its corners.

CHAPTER 8: Pattern Stitches

Most crochet fabrics are not actually comprised of rows or rounds of a single stitch. The open lace and infinite textures that characterize crochet are created by use of pattern stitches.

A pattern stitch is any regularly repeating sequence comprising combinations of basic stitches. Some pattern stitches are fairly simple and the sequence develops within a single row. Others are quite complex, with a repeated pattern both within each row, and one that develops over the course of several rows.

In this chapter, some other common single-row stitch patterns will be explored, and the project, Cozy Cowl and Cuffs, will put several pattern stitches to work. In addition, this chapter introduces the use of lighter weight yarn, looser gauge appropriate for soft, lacy fabrics, and techniques for the management of color pooling.

Single Crochet Pattern Stitch Practice Swatches

SINGLE CROCHET RIBBING STITCH

We'll start with the simplest pattern stitch, single crochet ribbing. This pattern actually only uses one stitch—single crochet—but the stitches are worked, row by row, in the back loop only, creating a corrugated effect. The resulting fabric is much more stretchy than regular "flat" single crocheted fabric. When not stretched, it's a bit thicker, and when stretched out, a bit thinner, than the regular sc fabric, as well. Often, the cuffs of sweater sleeves, the edging of a neckline, or the band area of a hat will benefit from a bit of stretch, and this simple pattern stitch is one way to provide that. When used in one of these ways, the sc ribbing is generally worked in relatively short rows, and then the whole piece turned on its side, so that the rows run vertically, in the direction that the cuff should stretch and bounce back. However, whole scarves, blankets, or sweaters can also be made from ribbed

WHAT YOU'LL LEARN . . . .

- How to make 3 different pattern stitches that use combinations of single crochet and chain stitches

- How to determine the multiple and decide on the correct number of chains to start with for each pattern stitch

- How to measure gauge in a pattern stitch

WHAT YOU'LL NEED . . . .

YARN

- 3 yarn scraps, 20 to 25 yds (18.5 to 23 m) each, worsted weight

HOOK

- H or I (5 or 5.5 mm)

- Yarn needle

- 2 stitch markers

fabric, making this one of the easiest ways to add textural interest to simple projects.

Here's the stitch symbol diagram for single crochet ribbing:

And here are the written directions:

Ch 21. Note: all stitches are worked in back loop only (blo).

Row 1: Sc in blo of 2nd ch from hook, and each ch across, ch 1. Turn. {20 sts}

Row 2: Sc in each st across, ch 1. Turn.

Repeat Row 2 to desired length.

Work a swatch of 20 stitches, for 6–8 rows, till the pattern of working in back loops only seems comfortable and familiar.

TIP Use "negative ease" to make ribbings snug. If a sleeve cuff needs to go snugly around a 9" (23 cm) wrist, the unstretched piece, as crocheted, might only need to be 7½" (19 cm) in length, depending on the inherent stretch in the yarn.

Both strips consist of 15 rows of 7 stitches each. Top: unstretched, as crocheted; bottom: stretched.

GRANITE STITCH

A pattern stitch may go by different names in different generations or parts of the world. This stitch is also sometimes called "stepping stones." However, symbol diagrams help to determine whether two names refer to the same pattern stitch or not. This pattern consists of (sc, ch1) with successive rows worked in the ch-1 spaces.

Here's the symbol diagram for Granite Stitch:

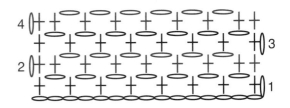

And here are the written directions:

Ch 16 (an odd number, plus one for turning)

Row 1: Sc in 2nd ch from hook, *ch 1, skip 1 ch, sc in next ch; repeat from * across, ch 1. Turn. {8 sc, 7 ch-1 spaces}

Row 2: Sc in first st and in next ch-1 sp, *ch 1, skip next sc, sc in next ch 1 sp; repeat from * across to last sc, sc in last sc, ch 1. Turn. {9 sc, 6 ch 1 spaces}

Row 3: Sc in first st, *ch 1, sk next sc, sc in next ch-1 sp; repeat from * across to last 2 sc, ch 1, sk next sc, sc in last sc, ch 1. Turn. {8 sc, 7 ch-1 spaces}

Repeat Rows 2 and 3 for pattern, to desired length.

Granite stitch. The top three rows have been worked in alternating colors, to emphasize the pattern created by working in chain spaces instead of tops of stitches.

PETITE SHELLS, OR MINI SHELLS OR SINGLE CROCHET V STITCHES

This is another pattern stitch with many names. It's a great one, by any name, for creating a solid but stretchy and soft fabric. In regular rows of single crochet, the stitches and strands of yarn comprising them, all relate to one another in perpendicular angles, reducing stretch and creating structure instead of softness. Taller stitches have more softening diagonals in them, but leave relatively large holes in the fabric between stitches. This pattern angles the single crochets on diagonals, providing soft drape and stretch, while still producing a solid fabric.

Here's the stitch symbol diagram:

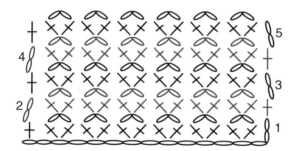

And here are the written directions:
Ch 16 (any even number, plus 4)

Row 1: (Sc, ch 2, sc) in 4th ch from hook (petite shell made), * skip next ch, work petite shell in next ch; repeat from * across to last 2 ch. skip next ch, sc in last ch. Turn. {6 petite shells}

Petite shells. In the top row, petite shells have been worked in alternating colors, to emphasize placement of shells in ch-2 spaces at center of shells in previous row.

Row 2: Ch 2, *petite shell in each ch-2 sp across, ending with sc in ch-2 sp formed by turning chain of previous row. Turn.

Repeat Row 2 for pattern, to desired length.

STITCH MULTIPLES

When stitches are used in repeating patterns, the number of stitches in the starting chain is controlled by the "stitch multiple." This term refers to the number of stitches it takes to complete one of the repeating sequences. For instance, in the diagram for the Petite Shells, it's fairly easy to see that each shell takes the space of 2 chain, and then the sequence begins the next repeat. So, the stitch multiple for Petite Shells is 2. This means that any even number will work—a smaller number for a shorter row, a larger even number for a longer row. But, in addition to the actual multiple of the pattern stitch, there are also usually one or more chains for turning (two in the example). There may also be one or more stitches at either end of the row that allow for stability in the fabric, straight edges as the rows progress, and also set up the base for the following row of the pattern. These stitches must be added, not to each repeat, but to the total for the row. In our example swatch, the row of seven shells at a stitch multiple of 2, means we need 14 ch, and we also need one for the last stitch of the row and two for the turn. In directions this would be expressed as "Chain an even number plus 3.

Common Double Crochet Pattern Stitches

The next few pattern stitches are created mainly with double crochet stitches and use a larger number of beginning chain, to keep the row from increasing or decreasing. The written directions for a specific project may only tell you the number of beginning chain for the specific piece being made. But a stitch dictionary—a book containing photos, diagrams, and directions for many pattern stitches instead of for specific projects—will always state the number of the multiple plus the extra chain needed for the first row's beginning, ending

WHAT YOU'LL LEARN..............

- How to read the diagrams and directions for three pattern stitches based on the double crochet stitch, and make swatches of each
- How to measure gauge in a multi-stitch pattern repeat
- How to read the diagram and written directions for a pattern stitch that uses both single and double crochet stitches, and make a swatch

WHAT YOU'LL NEED...............

YARN

- approximately 20 yds (18.4 m) each of worsted weight yarn scraps

HOOK

- H or I (5 or 5.5 mm)

and turning. The directions for the next few stitch patterns also contain this important information; and you can use any of these pattern stitches to create your own scarves, stoles, blankets, etc.

V-STITCH

The V-stitch, usually abbreviated V-st, consists of a double crochet, one or more chain, and another double crochet, all worked into the same stitch or space. The number of chains in a V-st varies according to the characteristics of the fabric being created. V-st makes a very soft, pliable fabric with medium-sized holes. It has a lacy appearance, a good amount of stretch and drape because of the diagonals, and is warm but still breathable.

Here's the stitch symbol diagram:

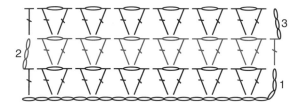

And here are the written directions:

Chain a multiple of 3, plus 4. The practice swatch shown below has a starting chain of 22 (18 + 4).

Row 1: (Dc, ch 1, dc) in 5th ch from hook (V-st made), *skip next 2 ch, V-st in next ch; repeat from * to last 2 ch, skip 1 ch, dc in last ch. Turn. {22 ch start = 6 V-sts}

Row 2: Ch 3 (counts as first dc). V-st in each ch-1 across, ending with dc in top of turning chain. Turn.

Repeat Row 2 for pattern, to desired length.

V-stitch. Row 4 has been worked in a contrasting color, to emphasize the placement of the individual V-stitches.

THE WONDERFUL WORLD OF SHELLS

There are innumerable pattern stitches based on the idea of working several dc in the same space, so the tops of the stitches fan out to cover as much space as a straight row, but in a softer, stretchier, more decorative pattern. Most shells contain an odd number of stitches, so that the following row's stitches can be centered, with identical numbers of stitches before and after the center of the shell. However, if more 2 or more stitches are going to be worked in the center of the shell, a ch-1 space is often substituted for the dc at the shell's center. This is because of that familiar offset between the stem and top of a dc stitch. When the top of the stitch is stretched out large by having 5 or so stitches worked into it, the offset is more visible, and the shell appears lopsided, with more than half the stitches pushed to one side and fewer than half on the other side of center. The problem is solved by using a ch in the midst of the shell, as will be seen in the first pattern stitch below, which is a simple Stacked Shells pattern. Our project for this chapter will use another stacked shell variation, but MANY other variations of Stacked Shells also exist, and there are whole stitch dictionaries devoted to the nearly infinite variety of shells.

STACKED SHELLS

Here's the stitch symbol diagram for the pattern stitch:

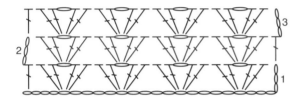

Here are the written directions:

Worked over a multiple of 5 stitches plus 6.

Shell: (2 dc, ch 1, 2 dc) all worked in indicated stitch or space.

Ch 26 (20+6).

Row 1: Work shell in 7th ch from hook, *skip next 4 ch, shell in next ch; repeat from * across to last 4 ch, skip next 3 ch, dc in last ch. Turn. {4 shells}

Row 2: Ch 3 (counts as first dc), shell in ch-1 sp at center of each shell across, ending with dc in top of turning ch 3. Turn. {4 shells}

Repeat Row 2 for pattern, to desired length.

Stacked shells. Rows have been worked in alternating colors to emphasize placement of each shell in the central space of a shell in the previous row.

STAGGERED SHELLS

Staggered shells is a pattern that produces a softly textured fabric without large holes. Because each row of shells sits between the shells of the previous row, alternating rows must begin and end differently, requiring two rows to repeat for the pattern. Each row does have the same number of shells, but in even-numbered rows, one shell is split, with a "half-shell" at each end. Because the following row makes only one sc in the center of each shell, the shells do not have a ch-1 space at their centers.

Here's the symbol diagram:

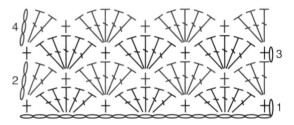

And here are the written directions:

Worked over a multiple of 6, plus 1 (with 1 additional ch needed for foundation).

Shell = 5 dc all worked in indicated stitch.

Ch 20 (18+1+1).

Row 1: Sc in 2nd ch from hook, *skip next 2 ch, shell in next ch, skip next 2 ch, sc in next ch; repeat from * across. Turn. {3 shells}

Row 2: Ch 3, 2 dc in first st (half-shell made), sc in 3rd (center) dc of next shell, *shell in next sc, sc in center dc of next shell; repeat from * across, ending with 3 dc in last sc (2nd half-shell made). Turn. {2 shells, 2 half-shells}

Row 3: Ch 1, sc in first st, shell in next sc, *sc in center (third) dc of next shell, shell in next sc; repeat from * across, ending with sc in top of turning ch. Turn. {3 shells}

Repeat rows 2 and 3 alternately for pattern, to desired length.

Staggered shells. The half-shells beginning and ending Rows 4 and 6 have been worked in contrasting color, to make it easy to see them. Note that the half-shells provide a straight smooth edge to the fabric.

In many project patterns using pattern stitches, the pattern sequence groups, such as V-st or Shell will be defined at the start of the pattern, in the section with stitches and abbreviations. It's important to read this section, because the pattern sequences will be counted like a single stitch in the rest of the instructions, and the directions will only tell you to "make a shell" or "work a V-st," etc., rather than instructing each component of the sequence. It's also important to measure gauge carefully in projects requiring fit. Often the gauge will be stated as "so many shells and so many rows = so many inches," or "so many pattern repeats = so many inches." Measure as normally, being sure to place the beginning of the measurement at the beginning of a repeat, and count the repeats as if they were single stitches.

Gauge: two shells = 2½"

CRUNCH STITCH

The final pattern stitch for this chapter is made by alternating sc and dc stitches in a row. When measuring gauge, each pair of stitches counts as a repeat. In alternating rows, the tall stitches are worked on top of short ones, and vice versa.

The fabric formed has a soft, nubbly texture, and because the posts of the dc stitches are bent between shorter adjacent stitches, there's a lot of stretch inherent in the fabric. It's a great one for socks, sweaters, baby blankets—any project that needs a fabric without holes and with stretch.

Here's the diagram for Crunch Stitch:

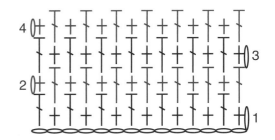

And the written directions:
Worked over an even number of stitches, plus 1.
Ch 15 (14+1).

Row 1: Sc in 2nd ch from hook, dc in next ch, *sc in next ch, dc in next ch; repeat from * across. Turn. {7 pairs of sc/dc}

Row 2: Ch 1, sc in first st, dc in next st, *sc in next st, dc in next st; repeat from * across. Turn. {7 pairs of sc/dc}

Repeat Row 2 for pattern, to desired length.

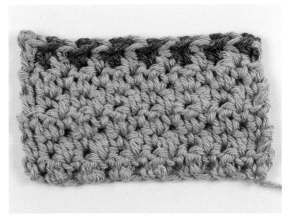

Crunch stitch. The top (6th) row has been worked in alternating colors to emphasize stitch placement.

PROJECT 8:
Cozy Cowl and Cuffs Set

Up till now, lessons and projects have mostly used worsted weight yarn. However, because of the structure of the crochet stitch, many fabrics that need to drape softly are often crocheted with finer weight yarns.

As mentioned in Chapter 7, the relationship between the diameter of the hook and the size of the yarn is an important factor in determining the drape and softness of fabric. To make an "average" sort of fabric, we've used worsted yarn with I or J (5.5-6 mm) hooks. When the fabric needed to have a slightly stiffer structure, a G or H (4.25-5 mm) hook created the necessary effect. In this chapter, the project will explore the other direction—using a large hook H or J (5or 6 mm) with sock weight yarn, to create a softly draping, wearable lace. At first, handling the finer yarn may feel awkward. It may be necessary to adjust the way yarn is held for tension and flow. Some crocheters find they need to wrap or weave the yarn through fingers either a little more or a little less, when working with finer weights of yarn. Experiment a little as you work swatches for gauge—but don't measure the stitches till you've worked several rows of stitches at an even, comfortable tension. It's probably easiest to start with the largest hook and the loosest pattern stitch, which are used for making the cowl. Then "graduate" to smaller hooks for the cuffs.

WHAT YOU'LL LEARN...

- How to manage tension to create soft fabric with thinner yarn and a large hook
- How to use pattern stitches in the context of a project pattern, to create a soft cowl and wrist warmers set
- How to recognize and manage "color pooling" in multi-colored yarns

WHAT YOU'LL NEED...

YARN

- 450 yds of sock/fingering weight yarn
- Shown: Cascade Heritage 150 Paints (75% Merino wool, 25% Nylon, 150g/492 yds). color 9804, 1 skein

HOOKS

- F or G (3.75 or 4.25 mm)
- H and J (5 and 6 mm)

NOTIONS

- Large-eyed needle
- Stitch markers (1 necessary, up to 5 optional)

FINISHED SIZE

- Cowl is one size, 14½" wide, 30" circumference (37 × 17 cm)
- Wrist warmers in two sizes: S/M fits wrist up to 6½" (16.5 cm) measured 1" (2.5 cm) above wrist bone. M/L fits wrist up to 9½" (24 cm) measured 1" (2.5 cm) above wrist bone

(continued)

WHAT YOU'LL NEED . . . .

GAUGE

- With F hook, in sc ribbing, 21 sts and 25 rows = 4" (10 cm)
- With G hook, in sc ribbing, 19 sts and 23 rows = 4" (10 cm)
- With H hook, in Stacked Shell pattern, 3 pattern repeats = 4" (10 cm), 5 rows = 3" (7.5 cm)
- With J hook, in V-stitch pattern, 6 V-sts = 4½" (11.5 cm), 5 rows = 3" (7.5 cm)
- Gauge is not essential for cowl, but is necessary for fit of cuffs. Adjust hook size as necessary to maintain correct gauge

STITCHES AND ABBREVIATIONS USED

- chain = ch
- slip stitch = sl st
- single crochet = sc
- back loop only = blo
- double crochet = dc
- stitch(es) = st(s)
- space(s) = sp(s)
- round = rnd
- place marker = pm
- move marker = mm
- V–stitch = V–st; in indicated st or sp, work (dc, ch 1, dc)
- shell = sh; in indicated st or sp, work (2 dc, ch 2, 2 dc) see diagram for stacked shell pattern below

COZY COWL

Notes

1. Stitch counts appear in {brackets} at end of individual row or round instructions.

2. Use of a blended yarn with 10%-25% (or more) nylon will add stretch to the cuffs. It is NOT recommended to use a non-stretching yarn, such as 100% cotton.

TIP Use stitch markers, every 20 or 25 ch, to help keep accurate count.

1 Make Main Section of Cowl

With J (6.00mm) hook, and leaving a 10" tail for sewing, ch 124.

TIP The main pattern stitch for the cowl, V-st, is worked over a multiple of 3, plus 7 chains. A larger or smaller cowl circumference can be made by working a larger or smaller number of chains, as long as it adheres to the multiple.

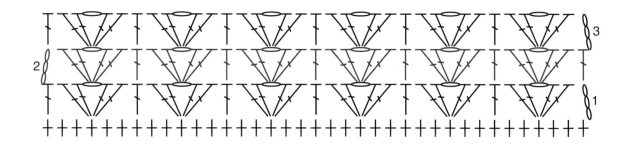

Row 1: Dc in 5th ch from hook (counts as ch 1, dc), ch 1, dc in same ch (first V-st made), *skip 2 ch, V-st in next ch; repeat from * across to last 2 ch, sk 1 ch, dc in last ch. Being careful not to twist work, sl st last dc made to top of first dc, to join. Use tail to sew first and last stitch together from join just made, to beginning ch edge. Work now proceeds in joined rounds. {40 V-sts, 1 dc at each end of row}

Rnd 2: Ch 3, PM in 3rd ch made , V-st in ch-1 sp of each V-st around, ending with a sl st to join final st to marked ch. MM to top of beginning ch of each rnd as work progresses.

Rnds 3–21: Repeat Rnd 2.

> **TIP** **Weaving Ends in Securely in Open Stitch Patterns**—To avoid having the yarn tails "pop out," unweave themselves, or create obvious trails through the open spaces of the fabric, make use of the fact that each crochet stitch has space at its center, hidden by the front and back strands. With the tail threaded on a needle, run the needle up through the center of a dc stitch, then up through the center of the stitch in the next row. This is the first direction—remember it takes 3 directions of stitching to make a secure finish. Next, run the needle under the base of a V-st, and then through the centers of the chains between V-sts. In this way, pass through 3 or so V-sts. This is the second direction. Finally, run the needle down through the centers of several rows of dc stitches, back toward the edge where the weaving in began. Tug the last stitch run gently, cut carefully close to the fabric, then tug the fabric a little to pull the yarn end back inside the last stitch it passed through.

2 Bottom Granite Stitch Edging

Rnd 22: Ch 1, sc in each dc and in each ch-1 sp around, ending with sc in beginning ch-1. Work now proceeds in spiral. {121 sc}

Rnd 23: Ch 1, skip 1 st, sc in next st, PM in ch-1 sp just made to mark beginning of rnd. Continue to MM to first ch-1 sp in each round, *ch 1, skip next st, sc in next st; repeat from * around.

Rnd 24–26: Continue to work rnds in Granite Stitch pattern (sc in next ch-1 sp, ch 1, skip next sc). At end of Rnd 26, sl st to join last st to marked ch-1 sp. Fasten off, remove marker.

3 Top Granite Stitch Edging and Finishing

Rnd 1: With right side of cowl facing (for right side, select the side that looks the best to you), attach yarn to opposite side of beginning chain, starting at seam joining ends of Row 1. Repeat Rnd 22 of bottom edging, working into loops at the bases of the dc sts.

Rnds 2–5: Repeat Rnds 23–26 of bottom edging. At end of Rnd 26, fasten off and weave all yarn tails in securely.

(continued)

COZY CUFFS

Make 2.

Directions for both sizes are the same, but use an F hook at stated gauge for the smaller size. Use G hook at stated gauge for larger size.

1 Make the Ribbed
Wrist Section

With F or G (3.75 or 4.25mm) hook (or hook needed to obtain correct gauge for desired size), leave a 14-16" tail for sewing, and ch 25.

Row 1: Sc in 2nd ch from hook and each ch across. Turn. {24 sc}

Row 2: Ch 1, sc in blo of each st across. Turn.

Rows 3–36: Repeat Row 2. At end of Row 36: Ch 1, rotate work 90 degrees, to work in ends of rows.

2 Make Hand
Section

Row 1: Work 1 sc in each row end across, ending with 2 sc in final row end. {37 sc}

Troubleshooting—Color Pooling

Some yarns are (often designated "variegated," "paint," or "ombre") dyed so that colors change at intervals. But different stitches use up each colored length of yarn at different rates, more yarn going into each dc stitch, for example, than into each sc stitch. As the repeats of each color "stack up" from row to row, it can either create a very attractive color pattern, or a polka-dot or camouflage effect, much less desirable in most cases. One way that crocheters can manage color pooling is to work swatches of different stitch patterns in a yarn before deciding that it's the right colorway for the project. The examples below show the same yarn, worked with the same hook, in different stitch patterns, showing, from left to right, less desirable and more desirable use of color runs in variegated yarn. A "rule of thumb" is that if the run of each color is just a few inches, the yarn will look best

Row 2: Change to H (5.00mm) hook, ch 3 (counts as first dc), *skip 2 sts, shell (see Stitches Used) in next st, skip 2 sts, dc in next st; repeat from * across. Turn. {6 shells, 7 dc}

Row 3: Ch 3, *shell in ch-2 sp of next shell, dc in next dc; repeat from * across. Turn.

Rows 4–6: Repeat Row 3. At end of Row 6, ch 3, join with an sc in top of beginning ch 3.

3 Edging of Hand Section

Rnd 1: Sc in each st and each ch-1 sp of Row 6, sc in each of 3 ch, sl st in joining sc. Fasten off.

Finishing
Using tail left at start, matching stitches, whip stitch together Row 36 and opposite side of beginning chain of ribbed section.

crocheted in an open, lacy pattern, with many chain spaces, to "spread" the color along the row. If the runs of color are quite long—often called "striping"—then a more solid pattern of stitches will still yield a pleasing result. The yarn in this project has short color runs, and the dc swatch shows the "polka-dot" effect caused by short color runs in solid crocheted fabric.

Gauge can also affect color pooling, along with its effects on softness and drape. These three swatches below, worked in another colorway of the same yarn, are worked with (l to r) F, H, and J (3.75, 5 and 6 mm) hooks. Note that the tighter gauge results in more distinct spots or areas of each color, while a looser gauge results in a more color-blended appearance.

CHAPTER 9: Multi-Row Stitch Patterns—Lovely Lace!

In this chapter, we'll explore stitch patterns that develop over several rows. Multi-row pattern stitches require careful row counting! Pattern stitches can be developed over any repeating number of rows, most commonly between two and seven rows per repeat. The practice swatches and project presented in Chapter 9 require three rows per repeat. This means that the directions and symbol chart will detail the foundation and "set up" rows (in which the pattern is established) and then direct that certain rows are repeated in order, over and over.

Chapter 9 also introduces a new stitch: the treble (or triple) crochet, abbreviated as tr in patterns. This stitch is one loop taller than a double crochet. When added to the arsenal of basic stitches, it provides a wider variety of options in stitch and row height, and adds much to the open, "holey" appearance of many lace patterns. When the treble stitch and following a repeating row sequence are mastered, you'll be ready to make the Chapter 9 project, a lovely triangular lace shawl. Let's start with the new stitch.

Standard stitch symbol for treble crochet (tr). Note 2 hash marks on the stem, as opposed to the dc symbol, which has 1 hash mark. Hash marks in stitch symbols denote the number of times to yarn over at the beginning of the stitch.

A New Stitch— Treble (or Triple) Crochet

The treble crochet (tr) stitch is very similar to the double crochet (dc), except that it starts with an extra yarn over, and is completed with an extra "yo and pull through 2 loops," doing that step 3 times instead of the 2 times for dc. The standard turning chain to start a row of trebles is 4 chain. So, to learn the stitch, start with a row of 10 sc

(ch 11, sc in 2nd ch from hook and each ch across). Just as in a row of dc, the first stitch is skipped, as the turning chain stands in place of that stitch. If necessary, the first stitch and last stitch of each row can be marked with stitch markers, as a reminder.

1 Yarn over twice and insert the hook into the second stitch of the row. Yarn over and draw a loop through the work. There are now four loops on the hook.

2 Yarn over and pull through two loops. Now there are three loops on the hook (A).

Repeat the (yo and pull through 2) two more times, reducing the number of loops on the hook by one, each time. After the third repeat, there will be one loop on the hook again, and the first treble stitch is complete.

2A

2B

2C

3

Completed first row of treble stitches, with turning chain to start second row.

4

Working into the top of the turning chain, to complete Row 2.

3 Repeat steps 1 and 2, working in each stitch across the row, until there are 10 trebles, including the turning ch-4 at the start of the row. Chain 4 to start the next row, marking the 4th chain (top of the turning chain) if necessary, as a reminder to count it as a stitch and work a stitch in that spot in the following row.

4 Work several more rows, until the stitch is familiar and comfortable.

Multi-Row Pattern Repeat Practice Swatch

Having mastered the basic stitches, the two most important factors to keep in mind now, are remembering to start each row with the correct number of turning chain, and whether to work in or to skip the first stitch of the row. The number of turning chain will always be stated in

a well-written pattern. The number of chain may differ, depending on the first stitch of the row, and whether the turning chain is to be counted as a single stitch, or as a tall stitch and length of additional chain. Our practice swatch will be worked in solid rows, each consisting of only one stitch type, so the only issue is to remember to work in the first stitch if making single crochet and to skip the first stitch and work in the turning chain at the end, if the stitches are double or treble crochets. Treble stitches in any row are counted in the same manner as double crochets: either count the sideways Vs at the tops of the stitches, or count the vertical posts. The post has two diagonal twists on its right side, and three small bumpy knots on its reverse or "wrong" side. In the swatch, the fabric is reversible, with each kind of stitch appearing as both right side and wrong side rows in the progression.

Troubleshooting

If after several rows, there are more or fewer stitches per row than the ten you started with, check to make sure the first stitch of each row is skipped, and that a stitch is worked in the top of the turning chain at the end of each row. See page 56.

The most common difficulty particular to the treble stitch, is that often the last loop worked off the hook, which forms the top of the stitch, ends up much larger than the others, as seen here:

Hold the loops closely together while working them.

It's not that the whole stitch is too loose, but just the top, and it can be very frustrating! The answer lies in managing the loops on the hook, while the stitch is being worked. The problem results from there being too much space between the loops on the hook, which includes extra yarn in the stitch:

Another cause of "big top syndrome" is tension irregularity as the stitch is worked. If the left hand does not allow enough yarn to flow into the stitch at each (yo and pull through 2) stage, but comes through with a very small and tight loop, all the tension of the stitch is at its base, and the top gets very loose. Conversely, if each loop is pulled through with a generous amount of yarn, it tends to use up the yarn in the loops on the hook, resulting in a small and appropriate top loop.

Left hand properly allows the hook to pull a generous amount of yarn through each time the (yo and pull through 2) phase is worked.

It may seem counterintuitive, but the more yarn the left hand allows into the stitch, as loops are pulled through generously, the tighter the top of the stitch becomes!

Only practice will enable the hands to complete the stitch with consistent tension! Work at least ten rows of trebles, paying attention to tension and to keeping the loops gathered together on the hook.

Note that the loops are widely spread on the hook, leading to extra space in the top of the stitch.

WHAT YOU'LL LEARN...............

- How to appropriately vary turning chain length for different stitches
- How to keep track of rows in a multi-row pattern repeat
- Confidence and familiarity with switching between familiar and new stitches

WHAT YOU'LL NEED...............

YARN

- 20 yds (18.4 m) or so of scrap yarn, worsted weight

HOOK

- Size G7 (4.5 mm) or H (5 mm), whichever is most comfortable

NOTIONS

- 2 stitch markers for top of turning chain and last stitch in row(optional)

Stitch Symbol Diagram

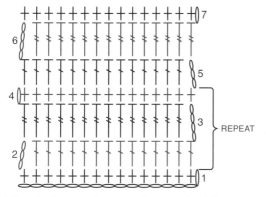

Work from the diagram, the written directions that follow, or both, depending on personal preference. Note that the diagram's placement of turning chains is a reminder of whether or not to count the turning chain as the first stitch of each row.

1 Foundation:
Ch 16.

Row 1: Sc in 2nd ch from hook and in each ch across. Turn. {15 sts}

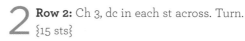

Completed swatch with arrows marking sc rows to make counting repeats easier.

2 Row 2: Ch 3, dc in each st across. Turn. {15 sts}

Row 3: Ch 4, tr in each st across. Turn. {15 sts}

Row 4: Ch 1, sc in each st across. Turn. {15 sts}

Repeat Rows 2–4 for pattern. Make your swatch at least 4 full repeats (13 rows). To keep track of the row being worked, it helps to use a small sticky note. Position this marker on the pattern directions indicating the current row, and then move it at the start of each row. The number of completed repeats can be penciled onto the paper marker.

BONUS PROJECT IDEA

Use the swatch pattern, make a summer scarf! Use yarn with a slight sheen and some cotton or bamboo fiber content, and whatever size hook makes a loose, light, and lacy fabric. (This will vary depending on the yarn. The example is stitched in "Spa" by Naturally Caron, with a G7 (4.5 mm) hook.) Continue repeating the pattern until the piece is as long as you want. Refer to Chapter 5 for a refresher on fringe options, or leave the single crochet ends flat!

PROJECT 9: Windflower Shawlette

Whether worn to warm shoulders on a breezy evening, or to welcome the change of seasons as a softly draping scarf, the Windflower Shawlette provides opportunity to use many of the stitches learned so far, and to practice a multi-row pattern stitch. This little shawl (or large scarf) shows what can be done with fine weight yarn, a large hook, and a pattern that repeats over three rows. For luster and drape, choose a yarn with fine texture, blending another natural fiber with some silk, rayon, or bamboo. And don't worry if the project looks bunchy and lumpy while in process; the magic of blocking will "open up" the lace, as long as natural fibers make up most of the fiber content.

WHAT YOU'LL LEARN

- How to wind a skein of yarn into a ball, by hand or with swift and ball winder
- How to make a triangular lace shawl of any size, starting at the bottom tip
- How to follow a multi-stitch, multi-row lace pattern, in both written and diagram formats
- How to block a lace project by the "soak and pin out" method of wet blocking

WHAT YOU'LL NEED

YARN

- 435 yds (400.2 m) fingering weight or lace weight merino/silk blend
- Shown: Valley Yarns Charlemont (WEBS) (60% Fine Superwash Merino; 20% Mulberry Silk, 20% Polyamide; 100 g/439 yds) Burgundy

HOOK

- J (6 mm)

NOTIONS

- Large-eyed yarn needle
- One stitch marker

GAUGE

- Gauge is not important for this project, but it's important to use a relatively large and loose gauge, in order to get proper drape and softness in the finished fabric. Gauge in the sample, before blocking, in sc rows: 15 sts = 4" (10 cm), Rows 1–9 of pattern = 4" (10 cm) in height

STITCHES AND ABBREVIATIONS USED

- chain = ch
- single crochet = sc
- double crochet = dc
- treble crochet = tr
- shell = sh: work 5 tr in indicated stitch
- stitch(es) = st(s)
- space(s) = sp(s)
- round = rnd

SHAWLETTE INSTRUCTIONS

Notes

1. Stitch counts follow row directions, in {brackets}.

2. Ch 4 at the beginning of any row counts as first treble st of the row.

3. Optional: Use a stitch marker in the 4th ch of ch-4 row beginnings, to mark top of turning chain.

4. Optional: Use a sticky note to keep track of diagram or written pattern rows as they are worked.

5. Finished size is flexible, and the shawlette can be made in any size, as desired. Sample is made with 1 skein of yarn. To make a full-sized shawl, work extra rows until desired size is reached. To make a kerchief or headscarf, work fewer rows, and follow the bonus instructions for edging ties.

1 Preparing the Yarn

Yarn purchased in a loose hank or skein must be wound into a ball or cake before beginning to crochet. You may wonder why many of the finer yarns are sold in this format, requiring an extra step of preparation! Commercially wound yarns often contain serious tangles at their centers.

While it's inconvenient to have to untangle the yarn, sturdy yarns made of mostly synthetic fibers are not harmed by the process. On the other hand, delicate fibers, such as silk or alpaca; or yarn that has been spun with haloed or bouclé texture can be seriously damaged by the untangling process. In addition, sitting for months on a shelf can stretch natural fibers, reducing the beauty and function of the yarn when it's used. To avoid these problems, many natural fiber yarns, fine and textured yarns, and other higher quality yarns are sold in loosely wound hanks or skeins

Yarn purchased for future use should be stored in skein form, to avoid stretching out the fibers by winding and leaving the wound balls to sit for more than a few weeks. When ready to use yarn purchased in skein form, there are two methods commonly used for winding: by hand or with a pair of tools called a swift and a ball winder.

Winding by Hand

To wind by hand, remove the label from the skein of yarn and open the large loop, carefully removing any threads used to keep the skein's strands untangled. Locate one end of the yarn, and let it hang free.

Drape the skein of yarn over the back of a chair, or the hands of a partner. Ideally, the distance should be wide enough to keep the strands of yarn snug—neither stretched tightly nor sagging loosely.

> ### QUICK REFERENCE
>
> Hank and Skein are interchangeable words that refer to loosely wound lengths of yarn, whether twisted for safety, or hanging loosely in a large single loop. "Pull skeins" have already been wound by the manufacturer so that the yarn is ready to use, either from the center or the outside.
>
>

Unwind a yard or so of the yarn, and wind it around three fingers, about 20 times around.

Remove the yarn from fingers, and fold the grouped loops in half. Now continue to wrap, but across the grain, perpendicular to the direction of the first set of wraps.

As the ball grows, turn from time to time, to wrap in another direction. Continue until the entire skein is wound into a ball. The ball will be used from the outside. To avoid its natural tendency to roll around, place the ball in a bowl when crocheting with it.

2 Triangle, Starting at Bottom Point

Foundation: Ch 5, 4 tr in first ch made. {5 tr (shell)}

Row 1: Ch 1, sc in each st across. Turn. {5 sc}

Row 2: Ch 1, sc in first sc, *ch 3, skip 1 st, sc in next st; repeat from * one more time. Turn. {3 sc, 2 ch-3 arches}

Row 3: Ch 4, 4 tr in first st (first shell made), *dc in next sc, sh in next sc; repeat from * across. Turn. {2 shells, 1 dc}

Row 4: Ch 1, sc in each st across, including top of ch-4 turning ch. Turn. {11 sc}

Row 5: Ch 1, sc in first sc, (ch 3, sk 1 st, sc in next st) twice, sc in each of next 2 sts, (ch 3, sk 1 st, sc in next st) twice. Turn. {4 ch-3 arches, 7 sc}

Row 6: Repeat Row 3, working one additional shell. {3 shells, 2 dc}

Row 7: Repeat Row 4. {17 sc}

Row 8: Ch 1, sc in first sc, (ch 3, sk 1 st, sc in next st) twice, *sc in each of next 2 sts, (ch 3, sk 1 st, sc in next st) twice; repeat from * across. Turn. {6 ch-3 arches, 11 sc}

Repeat Rows 6, 7, and 8, working one additional shell each time the sequence is repeated. Shell counts are as follows:

Row 9 = 4 shells
Row 12 = 5 shells
Row 15 = 6 shells, etc.
Row 30 = 11 shells
Row 45 = 16 shells
Row 57 = 20 shells

Sample was worked to a width of 20 shells, leaving enough yarn on one skein of Charlemont to work the edging. At end of Row 57, or at desired size, do not fasten off.

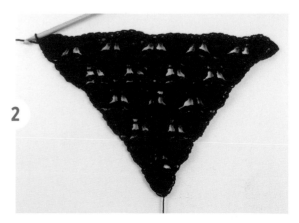

2

(continued)

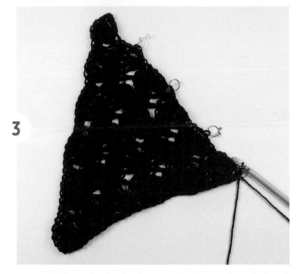

3

First side of triangle edge has been worked, tip stitch marked, and second side marked off in fourths for even spacing.

TIP When any pattern directs that a certain number of stitches be "evenly spaced" along an edge, there is a simple method for working the correct number of stitches. Fold the edge in half and mark the center stitch. Fold each half in half and mark the stitches at each fold. Now the edge is divided into fourths. Longer edges may require more divisions; shorter edges require fewer. Next, if the edge is divided into fourths, simply work ¼ the total number of stitches before reaching the first marker, ½ before the second marker, etc. In the current example, there will be 25 stitches between each set of markers. The marked "tip" stitch is not part of that count. Working the correct number of stitches in the first marked section is the hardest, but once accomplished, it gives a "feel" or sense for how closely together the stitches need to be worked.

3 Shawlette Edging

Rnd 1: Turn the work and repeat Row 4 one more time, working a row of sc across the top of the triangle. Rotate the work when the side edge is reached. Now work down the row ends, working around, rather than into the stitches.

Ch 1, work 1 more sc in the same stitch, and then space 100 loosely crocheted sc evenly down the side of the triangle to the point of the triangle, if the triangle is exactly 57 rows. If the triangle is more or fewer pattern repeats, be sure to work this round so that the number of stitches down the side of the triangle is a multiple of 8, plus 4 (8 × 12 = 96, + 4 = 100).

In the point of the triangle, the base of the foundation shell (the first shell worked in foundation step above) work 3 sc. Mark the center sc of these 3. Evenly space 100 stitches (or the correct multiple of 8 + 4 for the number of rows), up the final side of the triangle.

This first edging round sets up the base for the decorative border, so take time to make sure the stitch count has the correct multiple. When each diagonal side of the triangle has 100 sc and there are 3 sc at the point, turn.

Rnd 2: Ch 1, sc in first st, *ch 5, sk 3 sts, sc in next st*; repeat from * to * 24 more times, ch 7, skip marked "tip" stitch, sc in next st, repeat from * to * 24 times, ch 2, dc in final sc, making last arch finish with hook at top center of arch. Turn. {25 ch-5 arches on each side, 1 ch-7 arch at tip}

Rnd 3: Ch 1, sc in same arch, *(3 dc, ch 3, 3 dc) in next arch, sc in next arch; repeat from * 11 more times, in ch-7 arch at tip, work (5 dc, ch 3, 5 dc), sc in next arch, **(3 dc, ch 3, 3 dc) in next arch, sc in next arch; repeat from ** across. Fasten off.

4 Finishing

Weave in all ends securely. Block by soaking in a wool-soak product or water/vinegar solution.

Wet Blocking
Lace always benefits from being "opened" by first thoroughly wetting the fibers and then stretching out the stitches, allowing the fabric to dry under tension. In the steps that follow, a smaller sample is used to show wet blocking.

A. Place the completed shawlette in a large bowl or tub, and fill with cool water and the manufacturer's recommended amount of non-rinse wool soak. Alternatively, 1 tablespoon of white vinegar added to 3 or 4 quarts of water will accomplish the same thing, but with vinegar fragrance. (rinsing before proceeding to the next step will remove vinegar scent—simply repeat this step with clear water.) Allow the shawlette to soak for at least 20 minutes, but up to overnight is fine. It takes time for every fiber to fully absorb water.

B. Carefully lift the item from the water, squeezing out as much water as possible, but absolutely avoiding stretching, wringing or pulling on the fabric. Ball it up and squeeze! Lay the wadded item on a clean towel and discard the water.

C. Remove more water by rolling the item in a towel. Lay flat on the length of the towel and roll just like a wet swimsuit. Squeeze the roll by hugging it, to move as much excess water as possible from the item to the towel.

D. For the next step, any surface will suffice as long as it's clean, can be pricked by pins and will remain undisturbed for 24 hours or so. Foam "Blocking Boards" and "Blocking Mats" are available commercially, but many people use a towel-covered spare bed mattress, or the foam floor mat sections sold for children to play on. Lay out the item, flat, on the chosen surface. Starting at the center, gently smooth and stretch outward to the edges. When the item is flat and spread, start at one corner or tip (bottom tip of the shawlette in this case). Place a pin to hold the center of the ch-3 space at the shawlette's tip.

Continue working up the sides, alternating from one side to the other, spreading, stretching, and placing a pin to hold tension on each ch-3 space. These will become "points" in the edge of the lace, and greatly add to its beauty and "finished" appearance. Don't worry if several pins need to be re-positioned during the process. As long as the fiber is still damp, the pins are moveable. When satisfied with the even stretch of the item, leave it alone till thoroughly dry.

E. Remove pins; clip any yarn ends that appear, close to the surface of the fabric. The shawlette is now complete!

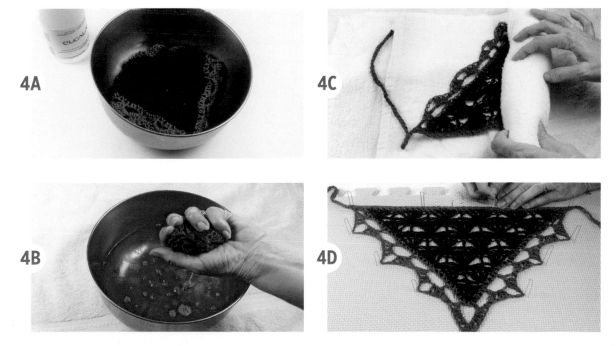

4A

4B

4C

4D

CHAPTER 10:
Surface Textures and…. A Garment!

So far, we've worked our stitches—whether single, double, or treble—into the top V of another stitch. But this is only one of the available options for stitch placement in crochet. We saw that working into the back loop only or front loop only of the stitch top created a slightly different effect. But many other rich and varied textures are also available: cables, bobbles, puffs, and other surface interest can be worked into the fabric!

This chapter introduces new ways to use the basic crochet stitches. We'll learn another ribbing method and the Basketweave pattern stitch, both of which use dc stitches worked "around the post" of the previous row's stitches. Clusters and Bobbles also provide texture, and are made by working several stitches together, in a manner similar to the "sc2tog" decrease worked in Project 4. When tall and short stitches are worked together in the same row, the taller stitches bend over, creating another variation in surface texture. (We saw this in the Crunch Stitch pattern in Chapter 8.) Now we'll explore the nubbly texture produced by alternating treble and single crochet stitches in the same row, in Seed Stitch. The project for Chapter 10 is a garment—a simple vest, open at the front, but with plenty of visual "pop" as it's made with many of the textural pattern stitches learned in this chapter.

WHAT YOU'LL LEARN. . . . .

- How to work both front and back post stitches
- How to use alternating post stitches to create ribbing
- How to use post stitches to work the Basketweave stitch

WHAT YOU'LL NEED. . . . .

YARN

- 30 to 50 yds (27.6 to 46 m) of worsted weight yarn

HOOK

- H (5 mm) or I (5.5 mm)

NOTIONS

- 3 stitch markers

Front Post and Back Post Double Crochet Practice Swatches

HOW TO MAKE THE FRONT POST DOUBLE CROCHET

The front post double crochet, abbreviated fpdc, is always worked into an existing row of stitches, never directly into a chain. So, start your practice swatch by making a chain of 21. Work a row of regular dc, starting with a dc in the 4th ch from the hook. You'll have 19 dc when the row is complete. Ch 3 to turn, and remember that this will count as the first stitch of the second row.

1 Insertion Around Post

Now yo to begin a dc in the next stitch, but instead of inserting the hook under the V at the top, insert the hook behind the vertical post of the stitch, from right to left. (Stick the hook into the

Correct insertion for fpdc

Loop drawn up to full height of row

Completed fpdc stitch

space between the first and 2nd stitches, across the back of the vertical part of the stitch and back out to the front, between the 2nd and 3rd stitches.)

2 Yarn Over and Draw Up a Loop

Now yo and draw up a loop—pulling that loop back the way the hook went in. Be sure to draw the loop through and up to the full height of the row being worked.

3 Complete the Stitch

Now finish the stitch like a normal dc: (yo and pull through 2) twice.

Place a stitch marker in the top of the stitch whose post was used, to make the skipped stitch top visible. It's located on the back of the work, just behind the post of the stitch newly completed.

Repeat Steps 1–3 for the next 2 stitches, making a total of 3 fpdc worked. Next work 3 regular dc stitches in the V-tops of the next 3 stitches in the row. Use the stitch markers already in place to be sure NOT to work in the tops of the same stitches!

Remove the stitch markers, and repeat the (3 fpdc, 3 dc) pattern, marking the tops of the fpdc stitches as necessary to help with placement of the first regular dc following each group of fpdc.

Repeat the sequence again, and the row will finish with 3 regular dc. The fabric now has a wavy texture, with the post stitches rising up toward the front of the work.

View from the back of the work after making 3 fpdc and 3 dc stitches

Placement for next fpdc, following regular dc stitches in the row

Completed row alternating 3 fpdc and 3 dc.

HOW TO MAKE THE BACK POST DOUBLE CROCHET

The back post double crochet, or bpdc, is made by the same process, but the insertion is from the back of the work, and the result is that stitches are pushed to the back, rather than pulled up to the front. Start again with 21 ch, dc in 4th ch from hook, and 18 more dc across the row. Ch 3 to turn, and start the post stitch row.

1 Insertion

Yo, and insert the hook FROM THE BACK OF THE WORK, between the vertical posts of the first and 2nd stitches, across the front of the 2nd stitch's post, and back through between that post and the next.

2 Yarn Over and Draw Up a Loop

With the hook head at the back of the work, yo and draw that loop back across the front of the post, and up to the height of the row being worked.

Hook inserted correctly for bpdc.

Loop drawn back across front of post, to the back and up to the height of the new row.

Note that the skipped top V of the stitch whose post has been worked, appears at the front of the work. In fact, it appears as if two stitch tops have been skipped, because the turning chain occupies the first space, and the bpdc the second.

3 Complete the Stitch

Now (yo and pull through two loops) twice, to complete the stitch, just as with the dc and fpdc stitches. Place a marker in the skipped stitch top.

Repeat Steps 1–3 for the next 2 stitches. In the next 3 stitches, work regular dc in the tops. Continue in pattern: 3 bpdc, 3 dc across the row.

Completed row of alternating 3 bpdc, 3 dc. Note that the back post stitches result in a horizontal ridge on the front of the work. This ridge is made of the skipped stitch tops.

PUTTING THEM TOGETHER— FPDC/BPDC RIBBING

Ribbed fabric stretches because of its texture, in which some stitches are to the rear of the surface, and some to the front. In Chapter 8 we made single crochet ribbing, which was worked "sideways" in relation to the rest of the project. Another ribbing, sturdier and less likely to stretch out (lose the ability to spring back into shape) is made with front and back post dc. It is worked in horizontal rows, so there's no need to turn the ribbing sideways to continue the project. The stitch symbols for fpdc and bpdc are these:

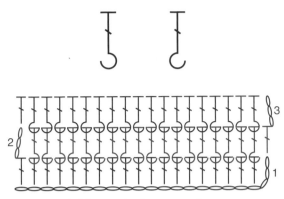

Here's the symbol diagram for the next swatch

1 Foundation:
Ch 22.

Row 1: Dc in 4th ch from hook and each ch across. Turn. {20 dc}

2 Row 2: Ch 3, *fpdc in next st, bpdc in next st; repeat from * across, ending with dc in top of turning ch. Turn. {9 fpdc, 9 bpdc, 1 dc at each end of row}

Row 3: Repeat Row 2.

Because of the way the rows reverse in direction, this row will maintain the direction of raised stitches—every post pulled to the front will stay at the front. Every post pushed to the back will stay at the back.

Completed swatch of Fp/Bp ribbing.

BASKETWEAVE STITCH

The woven appearance of this pattern stitch owes its texture to the reversal of post stitch order at regularly repeating intervals. In this variation, raised columns 2 stitches wide are alternated with columns of recessed stitches (with their horizontal bar on the front of the work), also 2 stitches wide. This pattern of repeats creates the appearance of vertical and horizontal bands. After 2 rows of that pattern, the sequence of post stitches reverses and the bands of raised stitches appear to dive behind the stitches facing the other direction. This is a great pattern stitch for warm sweaters and afghans, or for pads to protect a table from hot serving dishes. Like the ribbing, this pattern creates a reversible fabric and is suitable for projects that will be seen from both sides.

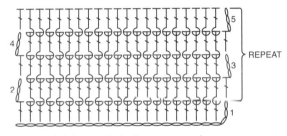

Stitch symbol diagram for basketweave swatch

1 First Set of Vertical and Horizontal Bands

Foundation: Ch 24.

Row 1: Dc in 4th ch from hook and each ch across. {22 dc}

The first 3 rows create the first set of vertical and horizontal lines in the pattern.

TIP Remember that in every row the turning ch counts as a dc stitch. The first and last stitch of each row will be a regular dc, with the post stitches starting at the second stitch of the row, and ending with the next-to-last stitch.

Row 2: Ch 3, *fpdc in each of next 2 sts, bpdc in each of next 2 sts; repeat from * across, ending with dc in top of turning ch. Turn. {5 pairs of raised and 5 pairs of recessed stitches}

Row 3: Repeat Row 2.

2 Second Set of Horizontal and Vertical Bands

Row 4: Ch 3, *bpdc in each of next 2 sts, fpdc in each of next 2 sts; repeat from * to last st, dc in top of turning chain.

Row 5: Repeat Row 4.

Rows 6–9: Repeat Rows 2–5.

Rows 10 and 11: Repeat Rows 2 and 3.

Row 12: Repeat Row 4.

A round or two of sc could be worked around the swatch's edge, to create a hot pad for the table.

Clusters and Bobbles Practice Swatches

Another way to create textured fabric is to use bobbles—raised stitches with a knotted appearance on the right side of the fabric. There are a number of types of bobbles. Cluster bobbles are created by the same process as the decreases we've already worked, and will provide lots of texture. Mini-bobbles are created by using tall and short stitches together in the same row. Puff Stitch is created by working extra yarn overs in designated stitches. Most of

The "woven" texture begins to be apparent as the second set of vertical and horizontal "bands" is completed.

TIP Because post stitches are worked below the stitch tops, they're not quite as tall as regular dc stitches. Many crocheters find that the standard ch 3 to turn, called for in patterns, is too tall and leaves loops along the edge of the work. To prevent this, ignore the standard instruction to ch 3, and make only 2 turning chains at the start of each row. All that matters in a turning chain is that it reaches the correct height for the row about to be worked. In any pattern, the standard turning chain is a suggestion, which can be modified to suit the individual crocheter.

WHAT YOU'LL LEARN..............

- How to make WS (wrong side) dc clusters in alternating rows of a fabric
- How to make puff or "raspberry" stitches in either side of a fabric
- How to use tall (tr) stitches between short stitches to create WS mini-bobbles

WHAT YOU'LL NEED..............

YARN

- Smooth textured, solid-colored, worsted-weight yarn

HOOKS

- Size H (5 mm) or I (5.5 mm)

these patterns are worked on the wrong side rows of a fabric, pushing the textured stitch to the right side. Therefore, the right side rows of the fabric are worked in plain row of sc or dc stitches. These stitch patterns show up best when a smooth-textured yarn is used—one without much "fuzz" or halo. It's also best to use a plain or monochrome colored yarn, rather than a variegated one, to enhance the appearance of textured stitches. Too much variety in both surface and color tends to confuse the eye, and make it difficult to appreciate the textured stitching.

Let's start with Cluster Bobbles, since the process of decreasing by working two stitches together is already familiar.

HOW TO MAKE 3-DC CLUSTER BOBBLES

The RS (right side) rows of the fabric can be any stitch—sc or dc are most commonly used. These non-textured rows form what's called the "background fabric" from which the bobbles stand out in relief. Our swatch will start with a background fabric of sc. After a few rows, we'll switch to a dc background, so the difference in drape and softness of the fabric is evident. Each type of background is appropriate for different sorts of projects, depending on function and appearance.

QUICK REFERENCE

Clusters or Cluster Stitches consist of a number of stitches begun and each worked to their last loop. The final yarn over and pull through unites all the stitches in one at the top. Clusters differ from decreases in that a decrease has the partial stitches made by inserting the hook into successive stitches, while a cluster's stitches all begin in the same stitch or space. Some older patterns denote a decrease by saying, "work a 2dc cluster over next 2 sts." This lets the crocheter know that the partial stitches will be spread over the space of 2 stitches in the preceding row, but will "finish" together as one stitch, reducing the number of stitches in the row by one. A regular cluster does not change the stitch count, as it begins in one stitch or space, and is completed as a single stitch in the new row. When the stitches comprising the cluster are taller than the adjacent stitches in their row, they bend outward toward the opposite side of the fabric, creating a bobble. Clusters may contain any number of partial stitches, and a well-written pattern will define its particular cluster in the "Stitches Used" section.

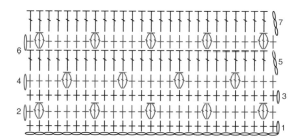

Symbol diagram for 3-DC cluster bobbles.

1 Start with a chain of 29 (multiple of 6 + 5).

Row 1 (RS): Sc in 2nd ch from hook and each ch across. {28 sc}

Row 2 (WS): Ch 1, sc in each of first 2 sts, in next st work (yo, insert hook and draw up a loop, yo and pull through 2 loops) 3 times.

(continued)

There are now 4 loops on the hook.

2 Yo and pull through all 4 loops—Cluster Bobble made, *sc in each of next 5 sts, cluster bobble in next st; repeat from * across row, ending with sc in last st. Turn. {5 cluster bobbles in row}

Row 3: Ch 1, sc in each st across. Turn. {28 sc}

Row 4: Ch 1, *sc in each of next 5 sts, bobble in next st; repeat from * across, ending with sc in each of last 4 sts. Turn. {4 bobbles in row}

Row 5: Repeat Row 3.

Repeat Rows 2–5 for pattern, ending with a Row 2 completed.

3 Without fastening off, let's switch the background fabric to softer rows, made of dc.

Row 2, (top) as completed—wrong side of fabric. (bottom) right side of fabric, showing bobbles.

A few rows of each background fabric should be enough to see and feel the difference. The sc background fabric is stiffer, thicker, and heavier than the dc background fabric portion of the swatch.

Row 1: Ch 3, dc in 2nd st and each st across. Turn. {28 dc}

Row 2: Same as Row 2 above. {5 bobbles}

Row 3: Repeat Row 1. {28 dc}

Row 4: Same as Row 4 above. {4 bobbles}

Row 5: Repeat Row 1.

Repeat Rows 1–4 to desired length for pattern.

HOW TO MAKE MINI (SINGLE STITCH) BOBBLES

The next textured stitch is also created from the wrong side of the fabric. In this case, treble stitches (tr) will be worked between single crochets, causing the height of the trebles to bend over and "bobble" on the reverse side of the fabric. By working these mini-bobbles in wrong side rows only, the texture appears on the right side of the fabric. Use the same sort of yarn and same hook to create this swatch, which again provides practice for the Chapter 10 project. This pattern is one of the ways to create what's commonly called "Seed Stitch."

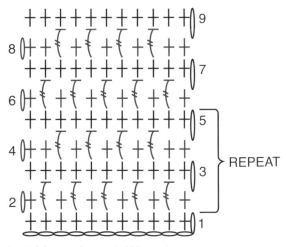

Symbol diagram for mini-bobble stitch pattern.

1 Start with a chain of 20 (or any even number).

Mini-bobble swatch after 9 rows.

Row 1 (RS): Sc in 2nd ch from hook and each ch across. Turn.

Row 2 (WS): Ch 1, sc in first st. *tr in next st, sc in next st; repeat from * across. Turn.

Row 3: Ch 1, sc in each st across. Turn.

Row 4: Ch 1, sc in each of first 2 sts, *tr in next st, sc in next st; repeat from * across, ending with sc in each of last 2 sts. Turn.

Row 5: Repeat Row 3.

Repeat Rows 2–5 for pattern.

HOW TO MAKE PUFF STITCHES

The final textured stitch for this chapter is the puff stitch. Like the others, there are many variations, but they all make use of extra yarn overs and extra loops drawn up, to create a thick, puffy stitch. Each pattern that uses puff stitches will define the number of yarn overs and loops to draw up for the particular variation in use. Unlike the other textured stitches, puffs show up well when worked in either right or wrong side rows. Use the same scrap yarn and hook as the other swatches in this chapter.

TIP It's much easier to pull through multiple loops if each loop is drawn up to the full height of the stitch! If the hook is catching on some of the loops, check to make sure all loops were made to full height, and that the chin of the hook is faced straight down, in the "6 o'clock" position as it is pulled through the loops.

1 Notice that all 7 loops on the hook have been drawn up to full height, and hook chin will turn to face straight down for the "pull through" step of the stitch.

1 Start with 20 ch.

Row 1 (WS): Sc in 2nd ch from hook and each ch across. Turn. {19 sc}

Row 2 (RS): Ch 3 (counts as first dc), in next stitch work the puff, thus: yo, insert hook and draw up a loop (3 loops on hook), yo and insert again, draw up a loop (5 loops on hook), yo and insert one more time, draw up a loop (7 loops on hook), yo and pull through all 7 loops at once.

Row 2 continued: *Dc in next st, puff in the next st; repeat from * across, ending with dc in last st. Turn. {9 puffs and 10 dc in row}

Row 3: Ch 1, sc in each st across. Turn. {19 sc}

2 Repeat Rows 2 and 3 for pattern.

In standard pattern language, the directions for this particular puff stitch would read: (yo and draw up a loop) 3 times, yo and pull through all loops on hook.

PROJECT 10: Stitch Sampler Vest

With an arsenal of textured stitch patterns, we're ready to create some really interesting fabrics! The Stitch Sampler Vest uses the Crunch Stitch (page 93), along with the textured stitch patterns from Chapter 10. It also provides a first opportunity to work on reading one size from a multi-size pattern, and covers some of the basics of garment construction. Choose three related colors of yarn, all the same fiber content and light (called #3, Sport, or DK) weight. It's best if the colors represent a light, a medium, and a dark value (page 63). (See Chapter 6 to review color values.)

WHAT YOU'LL LEARN...

- How to choose the correct size in a garment pattern
- How to read the correct size in a multi-sized garment pattern
- How to combine textured stitch patterns to make a Vest
- How to block the finished pieces to specific measurements, using a schematic drawing
- NOTE: The final edge finishing of this project will be completed in Chapter 11.

WHAT YOU'LL NEED...

YARN

- Sport (#3) or "DK" weight yarn
- Shown: Cascade 220 Superwash Sport (100% Superwash Merino Wool; 50g/136 yds), #811 (A), #1910 (B), #859 (C)
- Amounts vary according to size chosen
- Small: 3 skeins (A), 1 skein (B), 1 skein (C)
- Medium: 3 skeins (A), 1 skein (B), 2 skeins (C)
- Large: 4 skeins (A), 1 skein (B), 2 skeins (C)
- X-large: 4 skeins (A), 2 skeins (B), 2 skeins (C)

HOOK

- G7 (4.5 mm) or hook needed to achieve correct gauge. Because this is a garment, correct gauge is essential

NOTIONS

- 2 to 4 stitch markers
- Large-eyed yarn needle
- Measuring tape
- Pins for blocking

SIZES

- Small: to fit 32–33½" (81.5 to 85 cm) bust (finished bust 34" [86.5 cm])
- Medium: to fit 35–36½" (89 to 93 cm) bust (finished bust 38" [96.5 cm])
- Large: to fit 38–40" bust (96.5 to 101.5 cm) (finished bust 42" [106.5 cm])
- X-large: to fit 42–44" (106.5 to 111.5 cm) bust (finished bust 46" [117 cm])

(continued)

WHAT YOU'LL NEED . . . .

GAUGE

- 16 sts = 4" (10 cm) worked in Crunch Stitch (see Chapter 8)
- 16 rows = 5" (12.5 cm) in Crunch Stitch
- To check gauge, work a swatch 6" square (15 cm). Stitch count and measurements are before blocking

STITCHES AND ABBREVIATIONS USED

- chain = ch
- slip stitch = sl st
- single crochet = sc
- double crochet = dc
- treble crochet = tr
- front post double crochet = fpdc
- back post double crochet = bpdc
- back loop only – blo
- stitch(es) = st(s)
- right side = RS; refers to side of the fabric, not to direction of current work
- wrong side = WS; refers to side of the fabric, not to direction of current work
- place marker = pm
- bobble = dc3tog in same stitch
- puff = (yo, insert hook and draw up a loop) 3 times, yo and pull through all 7 loops on hook
- yarn over = yo
- Note: Stitch counts for rows appear in {brackets} following row directions

BEFORE BEGINNING—CHOOSING A PATTERN SIZE, CHECKING GAUGE

Most women's patterns are labeled according to "finished bust measurement." This is NOT the same as bra size! The correct way to find your actual bust measurement is this:

1. Wear the same sort of foundation garment as will likely be worn under the garment to be made.

2. Standing straight, with weight on both feet, wrap the measuring tape so that it crosses the largest part of the bust, and passes straight across the back, where a bra back strap normally passes. It can be helpful to have an assistant to ensure the straightness of the tape across the back.

3. Take a normal breath, with a normal exhale, and then note the place on the measuring tape where the "zero" end crosses the tape coming around the body. This is actual bust measurement. It's still not the "finished bust measurement" for a garment, though.

The correct and comfortable fit of any garment depends on ease, and the finished bust measurement consists of the actual bust measurement plus the ease of the pattern.

This vest is designed with 2" to 3" (5 to 7.5 cm) of positive ease; it will fit over a lightweight layer, such as a T-shirt or lightweight turtleneck. If it needs to fit over a heavier sweater, then it would be wise to choose a larger size. If 2" (5 cm) of ease will be enough, then the choice of pattern size is simple. Simply add 2" (5 cm) to the actual bust measurement obtained above. Look at the various sizes available in the pattern and choose the closest one larger than the actual bust measurement. For example, if the actual bust measurement is 34" or 36" (86.5 or 91.5 cm), then, the correct choice will be Medium at 38" (96.5 cm) finished measurement.

Having chosen the correct pattern size, note that for each set of directions throughout the pattern, there is a series of numbers from which to choose. Standard practice is to place the directions for the smallest size first, followed by the other options in parentheses. It's a good idea to avoid confusion by going through the pattern with a highlighter marker, marking the correct number for the chosen size in each set of directions.

Next, locate the section on gauge, and work a gauge swatch in the chosen yarn. The swatch should be about 6" (15 cm) square. We've practiced checking gauge in previous projects, but an actual garment is where accurate gauge becomes most essential. Choose the hook size that gives correct gauge, whether that's larger or smaller than the one stated in the pattern. Remember that the pattern only tells you what hook achieved this size stitches in the hands of one person—the designer. Each set of hands and each different yarn has the potential to affect the gauge, so use the hook that's right for YOU. After measuring gauge, it's a good idea to block the swatch, to find out whether it tends to stretch. Some yarns change size pretty dramatically when washed the first time according to label directions. Others don't change much at all. Remember, too, that the weight of the

TIP If necessary, refer to the blocking directions in Chapter 9. Stretching and pinning are NOT recommended for blocking this swatch or project, since it's not lace. Simply follow the soaking, squeezing and finger-shaping parts of the process. Measure the gauge a second time, after blocking and note the difference, if any, between measurements before and after blocking. The yarn used for the model did not change size appreciably (less than ¼" [6 mm]) in each direction).

finished garment will hang from the stitches at the top, pulling and stretching them over time. It's better to make a garment slightly short, if it's likely to stretch over time because of gravity.

1 Make the Vest Back Piece

Foundation: With A ch 58 (64, 66, 70).

Row 1: Dc in 4th ch from hook and each st across. Turn. {56 (62, 64, 68)}

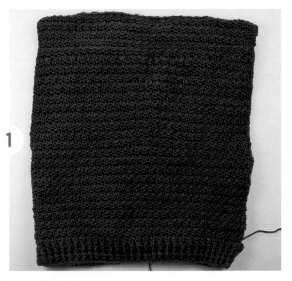

Finished back of vest.

TIP It's best to work the first row of each piece in the "back bumps" of the foundation chain—it creates a more attractive edge for each piece and can ease seaming and edging.

(continued)

Rows 2–4: Ch 3, *fpdc in next st, bpdc in next st; repeat from * across, ending with dc in last st. Turn.

Row 5: Ch 1, sc in first st, dc in next st, *sc in next st, dc in next st; repeat from * across.

Repeat Row 5 till piece measures 17¾ (18¼, 18¾, 19¼)" from from foundation edge. Fasten off, leaving 12" of tail for sewing shoulder seam.

2 Make Two Front Panels

The front panels are worked the same, except as specifically directed. They are constructed in vertical strips, starting at the side and working toward the center. Finally a side extension is worked, and a bottom edge band.

First Strip—Seed Stitch

Foundation: With B, ch 66 (68, 70, 72).

Row 1 (RS): Sc in 2nd ch from hook and each st across. Turn. {65 (67, 69, 71) sc}

Row 2 (WS): Ch 1, sc in first st, *tr in next st, sc in next st; repeat from * across. Turn.

2

TIP To be sure that all the pieces of the garment are matching sizes, it's a good idea to work the two front pieces at the same time. Having completed the first strip for the left front, make the same strip for the right front before proceeding to the second strip.

Row 3: Ch 1, sc in each st across. Turn.

Row 4: Ch 1, sc in each of first 2 sts, tr in next, *sc in next st, tr in next st: repeat from * across, ending with sc in last 2 sts. Turn.

Row 5: Repeat Row 3.

Rows 6–8: Repeat Rows 2-4.

Row 9: Repeat Row 3. Size S only—fasten off.

Sizes M (L, XL) Only

Rows 10 and 11: Repeat Rows 2 and 3. Size M only—fasten off.

Sizes L (XL) Only

Rows 12: Repeat Row 4.

Row 13: Repeat Row 2. Size L only—fasten off.

Size XL Only

Row 14 and 15: Repeat Rows 3 and 4. Fasten off.

Note: First strip should measure about 2½ (3, 3½, 4½)" (6.5 [7.5, 9, 11.5] cm).

Second Strip—Puff Stitch

Row 1 (RS): With RS of first strip facing, attach C with a dc in first st, *puff in next st, dc in next st; repeat from * across. Turn. {65 (67, 69, 71) sts}

Row 2: Ch 1, sc in each st across. Turn.

Row 3: Ch 3 (counts as first dc), *puff in next st, dc in next st; repeat from * across. Turn.

Repeat Rows 2 and 3 until whole piece (first and second strips) measures 4½ (5, 6½, 7½)" from foundation, ending with a sc (Row 2) row. Fasten off C. Note: Second strip should measure about 2 (2, 3, 3)".

Third Strip—Basketweave Stitch
Row 1 (For Left Front): With RS of piece facing, attach A with a dc in first st, PM for shoulder edge in this st, dc in same st (1 increase made), dc in each st across. Turn. {66 (68, 70, 72) dc}

Row 1 (For Right Front): With RS of piece facing, attach A with a dc in first st, dc in each st across, working 2 dc in last st (1 increase made), PM in last st to mark shoulder edge. Turn. {66 (68, 70, 72) dc}

(Both fronts worked alike from here on.)

Rows 2 and 3: Ch 3, dc in next 0 (1, 0,1) st(s) *fpdc in next 2 sts, bpdc in next 2 sts; repeat from * across, ending with 1 (2, 1, 2) dc. Turn.

Rows 4 and 5: Ch 3, dc in next 0 (1, 0, 1) st, *bpdc in next 2 sts, fpdc in next 2 sts; repeat from * across, ending with 1 (2, 1, 2) dc. Turn. Sizes S (L, XL)—fasten off.

Size M Only

Row 6: Repeat Row 2. Turn. Fasten off.

Note: Third strip should measure about 2½ (2¾, 2½, 2½)".

Side Extensions, One for Each Front Piece
At opposite end of rows from shoulder edge marker, measure 6½ (7, 7, 7½)" on opposite side of foundation chain and PM for underarm.

Row 1: Attach A with a sc in marked underarm stitch (this will be on the RS for right front and on the WS for left front); working from underarm down to lower edge of vest, sc in each st to end. Turn.

Row 2: Ch 1, sc in blo of each st across. Turn.

Repeat Row 2, till side extension measures 3 (3½, 4, 4½)". Fasten off A, leaving 28" of tail for working side seam.

Bottom Edge Band—one for each Front piece
Row 1(RS): With RS of bottom edge facing, attach A with a sc and work across row ends of front piece strips and side extension, evenly space 41 (47, 53, 59) sc. Turn.

Row 2: Ch 1, sc in each of first 2 sts, bobble in next st (see "Stitches Used"), *sc in next 5 sts, bobble in next st; repeat from * across, ending with sc in last 2 sts. Turn.

Row 3: Ch 3 (counts as first dc), dc in each st across. Turn.

Row 4: Ch 1, *sc in next 5 sts, bobble in next st; repeat from * across, ending with sc in last 5 sts. Turn.

Row 5: Ch 1, sc in each st across. Fasten off.

(continued)

Finished front pieces of vest.

3 Assembly

Assemble the vest using two of the seaming methods learned in Chapter 6. The slip stitch seam is used for the sides, since it's flat and smooth on the inside. The whip stitch seam is used for the shoulders, because it's the most invisible of the seams to use when pieces of differing colors are sewn together. In both cases, be careful to match stitches and work one seam stitch through corresponding stitches of each piece, catching one strand from each piece in each seam stitch.

Side Seams

With right sides together (wrong sides facing outward) match the bottom edge of back ribbing to the bottom edge of front bottom band. Using long yarn tail of side extension, and matching stitches, slip stitch seam to join front piece to back. Fasten off. Repeat for other side.

Shoulder Seams

With wrong sides together (right sides facing outward), match stitches at marked shoulder edge of front piece, to tops of final row of back piece. Work from armhole edge across first (Seed Stitch) strip and half-way across row ends of second (Puff Stitch) strip. One of the shoulder seams can be sewn with the yarn tail from the back piece, reducing the number of ends to weave in.

4 Finishing

Weave in all ends securely. The bottom front band and some other areas may appear "bunchy," refusing to lie flat.

As long as at least 50% natural fibers have been used, blocking in the next chapter will correct these issues. If an all-synthetic yarn has been used, the correct method is to wash gently and tumble dry on a permanent press setting, with gradually reducing temperature. Or wash and tumble dry on low heat, removing from dryer before completely dry but while still warm. Lay the vest flat, with finger shaping, to complete the drying process.

Note: Finishing will be completed in Chapter 11, with decorative edging for armhole, neck, and front edges.

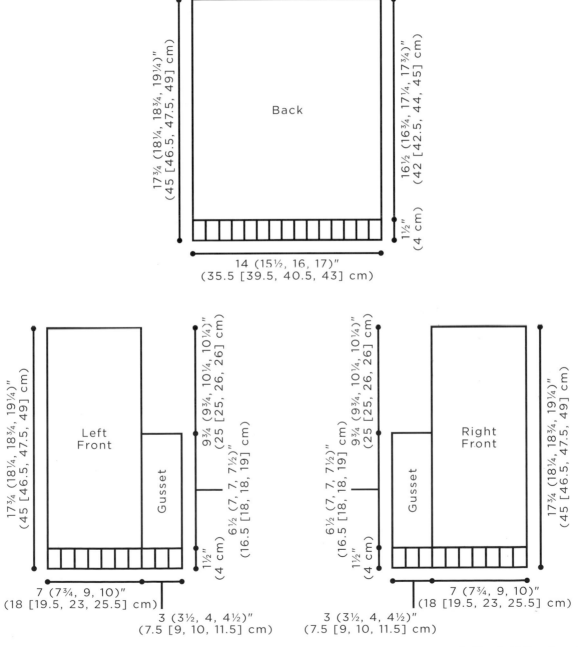

CHAPTER 11: Distinctive Details

The subtle difference between "homemade" and "hand crafted" in a finished garment, is often a matter of the finishing details.

Blocking, as we've seen, is one way to give good drape and a finished appearance to fabric. Another factor is "finished edges." Several projects have ended with crochet worked across row ends to provide a finished edge, but Chapter 11 introduces the Slip Stitch edging (for strength and to minimize stretching out of armholes and other areas that receive constant stress), the Reverse Single Crochet or "Crab Stitch", and the picot edge for adding a touch of elegance to any project. You'll choose whether to use the sporty Crab Stitch edging or the elegant Picot edging for the neck and bottom edges of the Stitch Sampler Vest, depending on individual choice.

Surface Slip Stitch

With the vest right side out, work in left armhole first. Attach A with a slip stitch under 2 strands of the first row end of side extension, where side is joined to back. *Ch 1 loosely, skip next row end, sl st in next row end, working under 2 strands; repeat from *, working across side extension. The chains between the slip stitches preserve the stretch of this side panel, end with a sl st in last row end of side extension. Now sl st in each stitch of foundation chain of Seed Stitch strip, up to shoulder seam.

TIP Make your slip stitches loose enough to be the same size as the other stitches of the fabric. If the fabric begins to crinkle up, it means the slip stitches are too tight. Be sure to pull the loop through adequately in each slip stitch.

Slip Stitch edging doesn't crinkle the fabric, but reinforces the edge to prevent stretching out over time.

WHAT YOU'LL LEARN . . . .

- How to edge an armhole with surface slip stitch

WHAT YOU'LL NEED . . . .

- Assembled Stitch Sampler Vest from Chapter 10

YARN

- 25 to 60 yds (23 to 55.2 m) of A, same yarn used for Vest project

HOOK

- Same as hook used to achieve correct gauge for Vest

NOTIONS

- Large-eyed yarn needle

At the shoulder seam, begin to work evenly across the row ends of the back piece. Inserting the hook under 2 strands of yarn for every stitch, simply work evenly, not worrying about exact placement. Space the slip stitches so that they don't ruffle (too close together) or pull together (too tight, too far apart) the fabric, but lay flat on the surface of the edge. This will work out to approximately one sl st for every sc row end and 2 sl sts for every dc row end, but the appearance is much more important than the count! The edging will be nearly invisible on the back, but will give a finished edge to the fabric. Join the last stitch to the first with a sl st and fasten off. Repeat for the right armhole, but starting in the same position, the direction of work will be opposite: up the row ends of the back piece, down the tops of the Seed Stitch strip, and across the side extension with chains alternating between the sl st in that final section. Join as before and fasten off.

Reverse Single Crochet (Crab Stitch)

Crabs are famous for their movement—scuttling sideways or backward, but never straight forward. This edging is named for that directional anomaly. We're going to work sc, but in the reverse direction. Crab Stitch does not leave a standard V at the tops of the stitches, because the stitches not only move "backward" across the row (left to right for a right handed crocheter), but are also "upside down," with their Vs at the bottom, against the main fabric, and a decorative bump facing outward and forming the edge. Crab Stitch can be a little tricky at first, but once mastered, is a GREAT edge to know. Many other edgings are too feminine for an item intended for a boy or man, or where a tailored finished appearance is desired. Crab Stitch is perfect for all those occasions, whether for garments, afghans, placemats, or other projects.

WHAT YOU'LL LEARN . . . .

- How to form the Reverse Single Crochet stitch (also commonly called Crab Stitch)
- How to work a Crab Stitch edging, including going around corners
- One option for edging the neck, front, and bottom edge of the Stitch Sampler Vest

WHAT YOU'LL NEED . . . .

- A swatch of single crochet, similar to the coasters in Chapter 2
- A swatch of double crochet, about 20 stitches by 10 rows

YARN

- Of same weight as swatches—worsted weight is recommended, with plain texture

HOOK

- Size H (5 mm) or I (5.5 mm) hook

1 Attaching Yarn and Forming First Stitch

With yarn on the hook, attach to the swatch with a slip stitch in the last stitch of the last row made. OR, use the same yarn, still attached to the last stitch. Pictures show the edging done with a contrasting yarn, but that's just for visibility. Chain 1, and insert the hook in the first stitch to the RIGHT of the attachment (2nd to last stitch of the row) (A).

Draw up a loop (2 loops on hook) (B).

Yo and pull through both loops. Here, a reverse single crochet stitch is being completed (C).

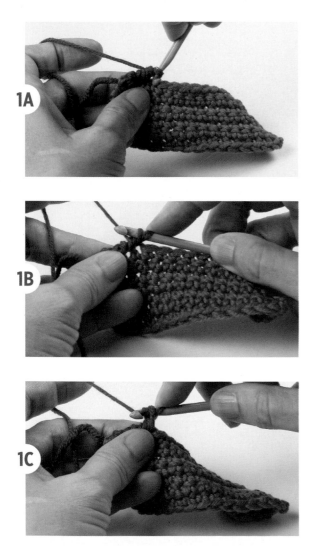

Completed first side of Crab Stitch edging.

2 Moving Across the Row and Around Corners

Insert the hook in the next stitch to the right of the just completed one, and repeat the process. It's the start of each new stitch that lays the recently completed stitch down, and forms the edging. Work across the row, to the right, making one rsc in each stitch to the corner (A). Best results come from working a little more tightly than for normal crochet, and at a slow, steady pace. This stitch is likely to get messy, with uneven loops, if worked too quickly. If worked too loosely, the fabric will ruffle (see Troubleshooting).

At the corner, chain 1, rotate the swatch and continue to work, placing one rsc in each row end. Because the regular sc stitches being worked into are not exactly square, many crocheters find that the Crab Stitch edging has a tendency to ruffle, as if too many stitches are being worked too closely together. The remedy is to simply skip a stitch every now and then, without working a chain . . . just skip a stitch and work the next rsc in the next stitch or row end. Do this as often as necessary to keep the work flat. At the next corner, ch 1, and continue to work across the opposite side of the foundation chain. Ch 1 at the next corner and work across the row ends. When you reach the first stitch made, turn the work so the beginning stitch of the round is to the left of the hook, simply join with a slip stitch and fasten off (B).

2B

Finished, blocked swatch with Crab Stitch edging.

CRAB STITCH EDGING ON A DOUBLE CROCHET FABRIC

The only difference when working the Crab Stitch edging on a dc fabric, is in spacing the stitches on the row ends. With your dc swatch ready,

follow Step 1 above, and again, chain 1 at the corner. As before, space the rsc stitches as needed, skipping as necessary to keep the edge flat. (see Troubleshooting.) Be sure to insert the hook into, not around, the dc stitches at row ends, with two strands of yarn above the hook to avoid stretching out the stitch. If rsc stitches are worked side by side in the same space (working around the post of the dc), they will not maintain their proper shape or spacing.

Picot Edging

The word "picot" (pronounced pee-koh) comes to us from a French root, meaning "little pricks" (little points). It refers to any decorative edging that has small points or loops evenly spaced. Picot edgings are worked in knitting, tatting, woven lace, and other fiber arts, as well as in crochet. The crochet picot is one of the simpler ways to achieve this ultimately delicate, feminine, and dressy edge effect.

Troubleshooting

Top: Stitches worked too loosely, fabric ruffles, stitches run together without definition. Solutions: use a smaller hook, work more tightly, or skip occasional stitches of base row.

Right: Stitches worked around posts of dc base row ends. Edge is not neat; stitches not evenly spaced, holes appear in base fabric. Solution: insert hook into center of each dc post for each rsc stitch.

Bottom: Stitches too tight and too sparsely spaced, fabric pulls in. Solution: work a little more loosely, skip fewer stitches

Left: Stitches correctly sized and spaced; edge is neat and straight, finished in appearance.

WHAT YOU'LL LEARN............

- How to form standard (3-ch) picots and grand or triplet picots
- How to work a picot stitch edging on a completed piece of crochet
- Another option for edging the Stitch Sampler Vest with picot edging, if desired

WHAT YOU'LL NEED...............

- A square swatch of sc, about 15 stitches by 16 rows, in worsted yarn with plain texture

YARN

- Of same weight as swatch for working edging

HOOK

- Size H (5 mm) or I (5.5 mm) hook, same hook as used to make swatch

FORMING THE STANDARD (3 CH) PICOT

At the right hand (beginning) side of the top edge of the swatch, attach the edging yarn with a sl st and ch 1 (or, finish the last row of the swatch, turn and ch 1).

Sc in each of the first 3 sts. Now the picot begins! Ch 3, and then sl st by inserting the hook down through the last sc made—put the hook under the front loop of the top V, and under the front "leg" of the sc stitch. This point of insertion prevents twisting of the picot, and keeps the picot positioned directly above the stitch to which it belongs.

Picot is closed or finished with a slip stitch through the front of the sc at the picot's base.

Continue across the row, working *3 sc, then a picot in the top of the 3rd sc; repeat from * across, ending with sc in the remaining stitches to the corner.

FORMING THE GRAND OR TRIPLET PICOT

In the corner work a "grand picot" or triplet picot: *ch 3 as at the start of a regular picot, sl st in the first ch made (3rd from the hook); repeat from * 2 more times, creating a row of 3 bumps.

These are the three lobes of the grand picot, but now the whole thing must be closed or finished, just like a regular picot, with a sl st through the front of the last sc stitch made (the base of the grand picot).

Grand picot closed with a slip stitch through the front of its base sc.

Because the grand picot is essentially an increase, it's a great way to get around the corner on an item being edged. Of course a plain picot, ch 1, sc, plain picot could be worked in the corner instead. The yarn used for the vest is finer, and so if picot edging is chosen, it will have a more delicate appearance than the practice swatch just edged in worsted weight yarn.

Because a picot edging has many of the characteristics of lace, it will definitely benefit from blocking. Swatch on Left is unblocked; swatch on Right was soaked in cool water, finger shaped and allowed to dry flat.

PROJECT 11: Finishing Touches

In this chapter, our project is to apply what has been learned about finishing details to the vest made in Chapter 10. The vest's armholes have already been edged with a sturdy and attractive surface slip stitch edging, but now a decision must be made for the remainder of the project's edges: Crab Stitch or Picots? Either is an acceptable option, and if unsure, try out one—if it's not "just right" for your vest, try the other.

When edging a garment, it's best to start the round in an unobtrusive place: back of the neck, side seam, or back of the bottom "hem" area. The vest has ribbing along much of the bottom edge, and we don't want the ribbing flattened out, so the edging will only run from the right bottom front up to the neck, around the neck, and down the left front side. In this case, then, the least visible place to begin the edging is at the right bottom edge. If a wider band of edging is desired, it's simple to work a round of sc all the way along this edge, then turn and work the "fancy" stitch final edge. If you choose to do so, be sure to work that base round of sc from the wrong side of the vest, so that the best side of the final edging is what shows on the vest's right side. Remember to work an increase at each of the top front edges. If picot stitch is being used, decide whether to do a simple picot increase, as described above, or to use the grand picot. If crab stitch is the edging of choice, then the corners will be worked the same as the corners of the practice swatch.

CHAPTER 12: A New Stitch, and More About Schematics

Having learned and used the chain, slip stitch, single crochet, double crochet, and treble, there is just one more basic or common stitch to know—the half-double crochet (hdc). Half-doubles create a thicker, more cushiony fabric than the other crochet stitches, and are great for soft sweaters, afghans, or (as in this chapter's project) slippers!

In this chapter you'll also learn more about custom fitting an item, through use of schematic drawings (such as the one introduced in Chapter 11) and working from measurements with careful attention to gauge.

WHAT YOU'LL LEARN

- How to form the half-double crochet (hdc) stitch
- How to work an appropriate turning chain for hdc
- How to recognize the diagram symbol for hdc

WHAT YOU'LL NEED

YARN

- About 25 yds (23 m) of worsted weight yarn

HOOK

- Size I (5.5 mm) or J (6 mm)

NOTIONS

- Stitch markers

The Half-Double Crochet

MAKING THE HDC PRACTICE SWATCH

Start with a chain of 16.

Row 1: Yarn over, insert hook in 3rd ch from hook, and draw up a loop. So far this is just like starting a double crochet stitch. There are 3 loops on the hook.

Yarn over and pull through all three loops. (1 hdc made)

Work across the row, making one hdc in each chain.

Turn the work and ch 2. Now there is a decision to be made, and it's purely a personal one. In single crochet, the turning chain is always 1 and does not count as a stitch—the first sc of the next row is made in the stitch immediately below the turning chain. In working double crochet, the turning chain is 3, and counts as a stitch—the first actual stitch being made in the second available stitch of the row. The half-double crochet has no such rule. The correct height for the turning chain is 2, because the new row of stitches is 2 loops tall. But whether that turning chain counts as the first stitch of the row or not is the "gray area." If it is counted as a stitch, that turning chain is noticeably thinner than all the other stitches in the row,

At end of the first row, there are 14 hdc stitches and a turning chain.

unlike the dc turning chain, which is almost unnoticeable when worked at correct tension. On the other hand, if the ch-2 is not counted as a stitch, the edges of the work will have a wavy appearance, rather than straight lines, because of the ch-2 loops at the ends of the rows. Usually, in patterns using hdc, the designer specifies at the start, which option has been chosen. However, that's only the designer stating his or her choice for this dilemma. While it does affect the numbers for stitches in the row in the pattern, it's by no means a law that must be followed. Many crocheters actually have come up with other solutions. Some people turn, ch 1, sc in the first st, ch 1 (for added height) and then proceed with the row of hdc, starting with the second stitch. This creates an actual stitch at the row end ... but it doesn't look exactly like the others in the row. However, it does solve the "problem" of the hdc turn. Another method preferred by many, is to turn, slip stitch in the first stitch and then chain 2, counting that as a stitch. It's still a bit thin, but stands squarely over the last stitch of the last row, and doesn't leave a hole. Other crocheters choose to ch 1 at the turn, pull up the loop slightly so the ch-1 is a bit taller than usual, and then work the first hdc in the first stitch. As you work your swatch, experiment with the different turning options, and

Rows 4–6: Ch 2 counted, holes appear because end stitch is thinner than others.

Rows 7–9: (Sl st, ch 2) counted as a stitch, no holes, but the end stitch is still "thin."

Rows 10–12: Ch 1, draw loop up a little not counted as a stitch, first hdc made in first stitch, no holes, straight edge to fabric, uniform stitches all the way across.

Rows 13–15: (Ch 1, sc, ch 1) counted as a stitch.

Bottom three rows: ch 2 not counted as a stitch, side edge loops evident.

choose the one that looks best to you with the yarn and hook you're using. The main thing is to be consistent throughout any given project and to remember whether the turning chain is being "counted" or not ... being careful, therefore, of the stitch counts for the row being worked in the pattern. However, it's good to remember that there are all the other options, because other yarn/hook combinations in other projects may require a different turning strategy to create a pleasing appearance to the work. The swatch below shows each of the turning chain options used for three rows.

Regardless of the turning strategy, there are some textural distinctives of the hdc fabric. It has a definite horizontal ridge that shows in every other row on either side of the fabric when worked back and forth in rows.

When worked in the round, the ridges are all on the wrong side of the fabric, and the front is quite smooth. That ridge provides extra possibilities for locations of insertion; many "fancy" stitches are actually variations on hook insertion in a hdc row. For the purpose of the Chapter 11 project, regular, top-of-the-stitch placement is what will be used.

Here's the diagram symbol for the hdc. It's similar to the symbol for the dc, but there is no diagonal slash on the stem.

TIP The hdc stitch has a larger offset between its post and V-top than other stitches. When counting stitches, remember that the post is below and to the right of the top of the stitch. When turned to work the reverse side on the next row, the post of each stitch is below and to the left of its top loops.

PROJECT 12: Any Foot Softy Slippers

These simple slippers are so versatile! Make them in infant size as a baby shower gift; make them in child sizes as holiday gifts; make them in lovely colors for sisters and girlfriends; make them in manly colors and larger sizes for the men in your life. Optional leather soles can be purchased online or at craft and yarn shops, and add durability to the comfort. They can be made in school or college colors—solid, striped, or color blocks! Only the size of your gift list limits the variety of slippers to be made!

WHAT YOU'LL LEARN..

- How to use measurements and a schematic drawing to custom fit a project
- How to choose the "right" hook and gauge for a project when not stated

- How to make comfy slippers for any size foot

WHAT YOU'LL NEED..

YARN

- 35 to 70 yds (32.3 to 64.4 m) of sport or worsted yarn for infant or small child sizes
- 75 to 100 yds (69 to 92 m) of worsted yarn for larger child or small women's sizes
- 150 to 200 yds (138 to 184 m) for most women's sizes
- 200 to 300 yds (184 to 276 m) for larger mens' sizes
- To work with doubled yarn, for added thickness, double the amount of yarn and increase hook size
- Shown: Women's: Cascade 220 Superwash (100% Superwash Merino Wool; 100 g/ 220 yds), ½ skein each, colors 887 and 1928
- Infant (page 139): Cascade 220 Superwash Sport (100% Superwash Merino Wool; 136 yds/50 g), 1 skein color 1942
- Child (page 139): Plymouth Yarns Select Merino Worsted (100% Superwash Fine Merino Wool; 100 g/218 yds), ½ skein each, colors 6 and 5

- Men's (page 139): Cascade 220 Superwash (100% Superwash Merino Wool; 100 g/ 220 yds), 1 skein each, colors 1945 and 1946, worked holding one strand of each color together

HOOK

- Size F or G (3.75 or 4.25 mm) hook for sport weight yarn (Infant sample slippers worked with G [4.25 mm] hook)
- H or I (5 or 6 mm) hook for worsted weight yarn (I [5.5 mm] hook used for child and adult sample slippers)
- J (6 mm) hook used for holding worsted yarn doubled, as in man's sample

NOTIONS

- Large-eyed yarn needle
- Optional leather sole in appropriate length
- OR optional "puffy" fabric paint for non-skid soles
- Measuring tape
- Pencil and plain or quad-ruled/graph paper

Planning the Project

In the last chapter, one body measurement was used to choose a pattern size. For this project, there are three measurements to take. Those measurements will be applied to the schematic drawing, and then gauge will be used to determine the number of stitches needed to achieve those measurements. In this way, ANY foot measured can be fit for the slippers, and you'll gain an understanding of the way patterns are designed. This understanding will free you to use a wider variety of patterns—sewing pattern pieces, with only minor modifications, can be used for crochet, for instance. One's own drawings can be used, too, if there is solid understanding of this relationship between the size and shape of the crochet stitches, and the use of schematic drawings and gauge.

TIP If making infant bootie/slippers as a shower gift, there is no little foot to measure! Newborn size booties or slippers usually have a 3″ to 3½″ (7.5 to 9 cm) sole length, and it works quite well to use the same measurement for #1 and split the length in half for #3. This formula was used to make the sample infant-sized slippers.

1 Measuring the Foot

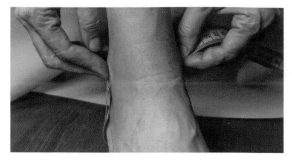

Pass the measuring tape under the heel, measuring from one ankle bone to the other, and note the measurement as "#1."

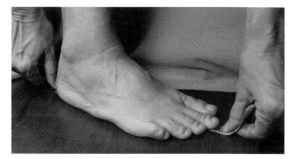

Measurement #2 is from the heel to longest toe.

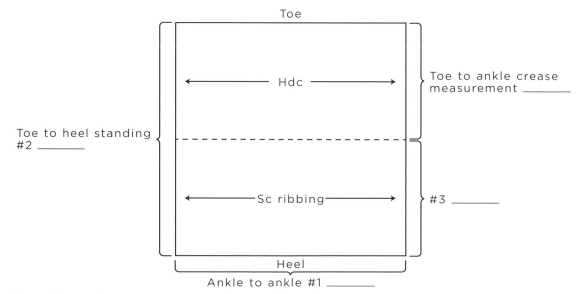

Schematic drawing with measurements labeled. Use graph paper or plain paper to make a drawing for your project. The lines don't need to be straight, and it doesn't need to be "to scale." It's just a tool, and a rough drawing works as well as a perfect one. Write the measurements taken so far in the appropriate places on the drawing.

The final measurement is the length of the top of the foot, from ankle crease to toe. Subtract this number from #2 and note the answer as #3 on the drawing. This gives the distance for the opening at the top of the slipper.

2

These swatches each have the same number of stitches and rows, all in hdc with ch 1 (drawn up tall) turns; they were made with the same yarn by the same crocheter. The size difference is entirely due to hook. Top to bottom: G (4.25 mm) hook, H (5 mm) hook, I (5.5 mm) hook.

2 Finding Gauge for the Project and Calculate the Length of the Foundation Chain

With the yarn you've chosen, work three different 10 stitch by 10 row swatches, each using a different hook. The three hooks should be the one suggested above for the yarn type, one slightly larger and one slightly smaller. Feel the swatches,

and look at them closely. Which one appeals most as a thick, soft, solid fabric?

Having chosen a hook, measure the stitches achieved with it. Count the number of stitches in one inch (2.5 cm) of a row. If there are 4 stitches in an inch (2.5 cm), and measurement #1 was 8" (20.5 cm), then it will take (4 × 8 =) 36 stitches to cover that distance. Of course the foundation chain will also need to include a turning chain. We'll be starting with some rows of sc in blo, so add 1 (the turning chain) to the total and you're ready to start the project! If there is a fraction in the stitches per inch, and/or a fraction in measurement #1 (4½ stitches per inch [2.5 cm] and 6½" [16.5 cm] for #1, for example) the multiplication problem here results in an answer with a fraction in it = 29¼. Simply "round it up" to the next higher whole number and work 30 stitches per row. Half a stitch can't be crocheted, after all!

3 Crochet the Rectangle with Tie Loops

Foundation: Leaving a 12 to 15" (30.5 to 38 cm) tail, start with the chain calculated in Step 2.

Row 1: Sc in 2nd ch from hook and each ch across. Turn.

Row 2: Ch 5 (for tie loop . . . how it works will become apparent when slipper is assembled), sc in blo in each stitch across. Turn.

Repeat Row 2 until piece is as long as #3 on the schematic drawing. Turn, but do not fasten off unless changing colors. If changing colors, fasten off here and attach the new color as the next row begins.

When the piece's length equals or is just barely over the "#3" length on your schematic, begin to work in rows of hdc, worked through both top loops of the stitch, using your choice of turning method at the end of each row. There is no need, in this part of the slipper, for the extra long chains at turning—we're past the ankle opening of the slipper.

(continued)

3

When the whole piece measures equal to or just over the #2 length (total length of foot), fasten off, leaving at least a 36" (91.5 cm) tail.

TIP If Stripes are desired for the heel section, simply work 2 rows of each color, alternating. Change colors in the last stitch of the second row of each color, and carry the other color on the same side of the work each time...this will become the inside of the slipper and the float will not be apparent once the tie strings are threaded through the loops and the slipper is right side out.

QUICK REFERENCE

A float is a length of yarn not worked into any stitch, but being carried along the work until needed again. Floats often occur at the ends of rows in striped work, and can run along the back of other work with color changes within a row.

4 Assemble the Slipper

Thread the long ending tail onto a large-eyed yarn needle and run a stitch along the ends of the row just completed, catching just one loop from the top of each hdc stitch. Pull firmly on the tail, and the end of the rectangle will curl up in a tightly gathered circle. Pull tightly enough that there is no visible hole in the center of the circle just created. Now make a small locking stitch by inserting the needle under the first and last stitch (the ends of the row, where they now meet each other). Repeat 2 or 3 times, for sturdiness (A).

With the same yarn still threaded on the needle, make sure that the slipper is facing wrong side out. This won't be evident if only one color has been used, but if stripes were worked, the side with the yarn floats is the wrong side of the work—the inside of the slipper. Make a whip-stitch seam (see Chapter 6 for review if necessary), joining the ends of the hdc rows. When the seam reaches the transition to sc ribbing rows, again work a locking stitch, as above, and fasten off.

4A

4B

(B) Next, thread the yarn needle onto the beginning tail, fold the foundation chain at the heel end of the slipper in half, and sew a whipstitch seam. Weave in all ends.

5 Ties
(make 1 for each slipper)

Chain three times the number of stitches used for the foundation of the slipper in step 2. Sl st in each ch across. Fasten off and weave in both yarn ends. This is the same method as used for ties in Chapter 4. Use the crochet hook to pull the tie through the ch-5 loops at the ends of the ribbing rows, so that the center of the tie is centered at the heel seam and the ends are at each side of the seam at the top of the foot.

TIP Ties can be made in the same color, one of the stripe colors, or any color as whimsy dictates! Once threaded, a knot tied right at each end of the tie makes it easier to use, and helps prevent the tie coming out of the loops in the laundry.

6 Non-Skid Coatings
for Slipper Soles (optional)

Ready made leather slipper soles are available online, or in yarn shops or craft stores. Purchase the size closest to the actual foot measurement taken in step 1. When the slipper is assembled, use the pre-drilled holes in the leather to whipstitch the sole to the slipper (A), being careful

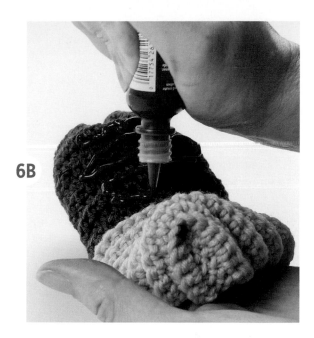

6B

to center the heal seam and top of foot seam in line with the end points of the sole. Slippers with leather soles are NOT machine washable! Follow the manufacturer's cleaning instructions for any leather item.

Alternatively, use puffy fabric paint, available at most craft stores, to paint "tread" onto the bottoms of the slippers (B). Allow the paint to cure in air for about 72 hours, long after it feels dry to the touch, for longest lasting results.

Infinite variety is possible when using this method of project planning! Measure, draw a schematic, find gauge, and voila—you're designing your own projects!

6A

Crochet Traditions

The first 12 chapters have taught you the basic skills of crochet. If worked through sequentially, all the basic stitches and techniques have been learned. The final section of Crochet 101 will introduce some of the traditional forms and uses of crochet, and a few alternate techniques. Chapters 13–16 can be used in any order— choose the techniques you'd like to explore and feel free to skip around, sampling the variety of forms crochet has taken!

With that spirit of exploration in mind, Chapter 13 introduces the world of thread lace, and offers a Poinsettia Doily as its project. Chapter 14 introduces filet crochet and the charts from which these lovely, geometric pictures are worked. Tunisian or Afghan crochet, the topic of Chapter 15, uses different tools, and offers a real change of pace from regular crochet. Chapter 16 offers tips and tricks to make crochet easier and the results more professional in appearance.

CHAPTER 13:
Introduction to Threadwork

With the arsenal of skills already gained, let's get started with an introduction to thread. Thread is spun much more tightly than yarn, and does not stretch or "give" when worked. This means that much tighter tension is needed, but also means that really intricate figures can be worked from the basic stitches.

There are several traditional styles of threadwork, including Irish crochet (characterized by three dimensional motifs joined together with mesh and loops), filet crochet, and flat crochet lace. This chapter will introduce the use of thread in Flat Lace. Because thread is worked at high tension, aluminum or bamboo hooks are not appropriate. They can easily snap or bend in use. Small steel hooks are generally used for threadwork. Ergonomic hook handles are available in a wide range of prices, to make threadwork easier on the hands. Both the threads and hooks are numbered for size in the same manner as wire gauges: the larger the number, the smaller the diameter. Working with fine thread and tiny hooks requires excellent eyesight or the use of a magnifying glass. Many craft suppliers sell a Crafter's Magnifier that hangs around the neck, between the eyes and the work, leaving both hands free. Excellent light is also helpful in working with very small stitches. Many people find it easier to start with a larger thread, such as a size 3 or 5 and gradually work down to the standard #10 used for bedspreads, tablecloths, and many doilies.

The only difference created by working with a thicker thread is that the diameter of the finished piece will be larger. Many doily patterns do not state gauge, merely assuming that the crocheter will use a hook appropriate to the thread size, and work tightly enough for the solid sections in the lace to really be solid. Here's a "rule of thumb" for matching steel hook size to thread size:

#3 thread or perle cotton: size 00–2 hook

#5 thread: size 3–7 hook

#10 thread, also called "bedspread" cotton or simply "crochet thread": size 5–10 hook

#20–#30 thread: size 10–14 hook

#40–#80 thread: size 14–18 hook

The demonstration photos in this chapter show #10 thread being worked with a size 5 hook. It will be evident that the basic structure for a round or other-shaped doily is the same as the motifs we've already worked in yarn. The center is the starting place, and following rounds radiate outward, using increases inherent in the stitch pattern. One difference, though, is that patterns often call for more increases than seem necessary in certain rounds, creating ruffling. Usually this extra will be taken up when a future round puts tension on those "extra" stitches or chain loops. Like all lace, cotton thread doilies require blocking when finished, but the method is different because cotton fiber has different characteristics than synthetics or animal fibers.

Threadwork was traditionally done in white and off-white (bleached or unbleached) cotton thread. However, threads are now available in a rainbow of colors and in many fiber blends besides plain cotton. The swatches and project in this chapter are worked in bright colors, to make them more visible, but feel free to follow personal inclination in making color choices.

WHAT YOU'LL LEARN . . . .

- Correct tension for threadwork
- How to make an alternate joining for crochet in rounds
- How to make a small medallion to use as a necklace or earring

WHAT YOU'LL NEED . . . .

- Choose a steel hook that you can see and manage

THREAD

- Use the chart to choose a thread size that will work well with the chosen hook

NOTIONS

- Medium sized (#17 approx.) darning needle
- Optional jump ring and necklace finding

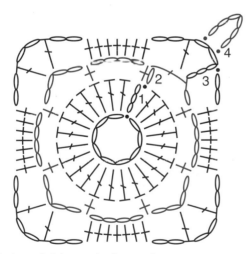

Here's the symbol diagram for this swatch.

> **TIP** It's fine to work the first round over the beginning tail. This will form the first step in weaving in. By itself, working over the tail is not enough to ensure that the piece doesn't ravel from the center outward over time; but it's a great start and shortens the "weaving in" process at the finish.

Thread Practice Swatch

1 Foundation and Round 1

Place a slip knot on the hook, leaving a 4 to 6" (10 to 15 cm) tail. Don't completely tighten the slip knot. Chain 9 tightly, join in a ring by making a slip stitch in the first chain. Now pull the beginning tail to tighten the slip knot. The join is the reason for making that first loop a little loose. Generally, when working with thread, the goal is to work chains as tightly as possible as they will generally be worked "around" rather than worked "into." It's a good idea to read through the directions for any round to find out if there are chains that should be a bit looser, and make them accordingly.

(continued)

Thread Practice Swatch (continued)

Next, ch 3 keeping the loops no larger than what will slide off the hook. Work 23 dc into the ring. Generally the beginning ring will hold 2 to 3 times as many stitches as the number of chains that make up the ring. The goal is to solidly fill the ring. Stitches should continually be slid to the right as they're completed. They should lie flat, side by side, neither overlapping nor having spaces between. Practice till a solid flat ring is produced. The beginning ch-3, as usual, counts as the first dc, resulting in a ring of 24 dc. Join the last stitch to the first with a sl st. Some traditional lace patterns begin with sc in the ring, or hdc or tr. It really depends on the structure and appearance of the individual design.

TIP When working lace with thread, listen for a very slight "pop" sound as the loop comes off the hook. This is a good sign that enough tension is present. Work for short periods of time to avoid cramps and other hand stress.

2 Building on the Foundation

Rnd 2: Ch 1, sc in the same st as join, *ch 4, skip next 2 dc, sc in next dc; repeat from * around, ending with dc in top of first sc (the dc counts as 3 chain).

When the following round requires a start in the top of an arch, rather than at its ending (left hand) side, an actual stitch of the required height is sometimes substituted for the last chain and join. {8 ch-4 arches}

Troubleshooting

Left: Too loose with ring showing between bases of dc stitches; solve by holding yarn with tighter tension.
Center: Stitches overlapped and worked over each other; they were all slid to the right at the end, when ring was full before number was complete.

Right: Stitches lying flat and even, side by side.

Slide stitches to the right around the ring after every 2–4 stitches are completed, to keep them "packed" neatly and lying flat, side by side.

1) Ch 1, dc (1 + 3 = 4), which puts the working yarn slightly right of center in the arch.

2) Ch 2, hdc (2 + 2 = 4), which puts the work right at the center of the arch, but has a thicker stitch making up part of the arch.

3) Ch 3, sc (3 + 1 = 4), which puts the work slightly left of the center of the arch, but the sc can create the appearance of a knot at that point.

The designer has chosen option 1 because it creates the correct length without changing the thickness or creating the appearance of a knot.

Rnd 3: Ch 5 (counts as dc, ch 2), dc around joining st as if it were a ch, ch 2, *7 sc in next arch, ch 2, (dc, ch 2, dc) in next arch (V-st made), ch 2; repeat from * around to last arch, 7 sc in last arch, ch 2, join with a sl st in 3rd ch of beginning ch-5. {4 V-sts}

3 Finishing

Sl st in next ch-2 sp, ch 6, sl st in same ch-2 sp. Fasten off. Weave in both ends securely.

Block medallion by pressing firmly with a steam iron set on high heat OR block by wetting thoroughly and pressing firmly with a hot dry iron. In either case, be sure to stretch out the piece, and be careful not to burn fingers!

3

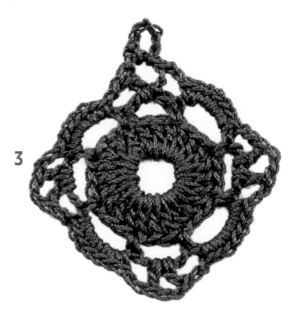

Optional: Attach jump ring to finishing loop and thread necklace chain through ring . It's also quite practical to attach a jump ring and fishhook style earring finding, turning two medallions into a pair of designer earrings.

PROJECT 13: Poinsettia Doily

This project is presented as threadwork; however, it can also be worked with an aluminum hook and fingering or DK weight yarn, for a different finished appearance. Poinsettias are a cheerful addition to winter holiday decorations; however, this little doily is equally attractive worked in two colors as shown, in white, or in a single solid color.

WHAT YOU'LL LEARN . . . .

- How to make a two-color thread doily
- How to adapt the same pattern for use with yarn

WHAT YOU'LL NEED . . . .

YARN

- 60 yds (55 m) each of red and green thread in convenient size
- Shown: "Sissy 10" (100% mercerized cotton, 50 g/280 m, size 10)

HOOK

- Of corresponding size for chosen thread
- Sample worked with a steel #5 (1.8 mm)

NOTIONS

- Medium darning needle
- Steam and iron for blocking

GAUGE

- Gauge will vary depending on thread and hook size. Work should be relatively tight

FINISHED SIZE

- Size will vary, depending on thread and hook size chosen. Sample measures 6" (15 cm) in diameter from tip to tip

STITCHES AND ABBREVIATIONS USED

- chain = ch
- slip stitch = sl st
- single crochet = sc
- double crochet = dc
- space(es) = sp(s)
- stitch(es) = st(s)
- round = rnd
- shell = Shells in this pattern vary from row to row and are defined in row directions. Each shell, regardless of size, has a ch-2 or ch-3 space at its center. Shells are always worked in the center space of a previous shell.

INSTRUCTIONS

Notes

1. Stitch counts appear in {brackets} following round directions.

2. Each round after the first begins in the center of a shell, and the final join of the round completes that first shell.

TIP Use a small sticky flag or arrow to keep track of the rounds as you work the diagram. Simply point the arrow to the start of the current round, and move it as the work progresses from one round to another.

(continued)

PROJECT 13: Poinsettia Doily
(continued)

1 Foundation and Set-up for Shells

With red thread, ch 9, join with a sl st to form a ring.

Rnd 1: Ch 3 (counts as dc, here and throughout), dc in ring, (ch 2, 2 dc in ring) 8 times, ch 1, join with a sc in top of beginning ch-3. {Nine 2-dc groups, 9 ch-1 sps}

Rnd 2: Ch 3, working around sc as if it were a chain dc in ring, ch 1, *(2 dc, ch 2, 2 dc) shell in next ch-2 sp, ch 1; repeat from * 7 more times, 2 dc in same sp as beginning, ch 1, sc in top of beginning ch to join. {Nine (2 dc, ch 2, 2 dc) shells}

2 Red Shell Rounds

Rnd 3: Ch 3, dc in same sp, *ch 4, skip ch-1 sp, (2 dc, ch 2, 2 dc) shell in ch-2 sp of next shell; repeat from * around, ending with 2 dc in same sp as beginning, ch 1, sc in top of beginning ch-3 to complete final shell. {9 shells, 9 ch-4 arches}

Rnd 4: Ch 3, 2 dc in same sp, *ch 3, skip ch-4 arch, (3 dc, ch 2, 3 dc) shell in ch-2 sp of next shell; repeat from * around, ending with 3 dc in same sp as beginning, ch 1, sc in top of beginning ch-3 to complete final shell. {Nine (3 dc, ch 2, 3 dc) shells, 9 ch-3 arches}

Stitch symbol diagram for the Poinsettia Doily—Rounds are shaded to help keep track. Note that each round begins with half a shell, and ends with completing of that shell.

Round 2 completed.

Rnd 5: Ch 3, 2 dc in same sp, *ch 3, working around ch-3 arch of Rnd 4 AND ch-4 arch of Rnd 3 work sc, ch 3**, (3 dc, ch 2, 3 dc) in next shell; repeat from * around ending at **, 3 dc in same sp as beginning, ch 2 and sl st to join to complete final shell. Fasten off red thread. {Nine (3 dc, ch 2, 3 dc) shells, 9 sc}

2

Round 3 will appear to "ruffle," as if there are too many chains between shells. This "slack" will be taken up later, in Round 5.

2

Work the sc as tightly as possible, drawing the chain arches together.

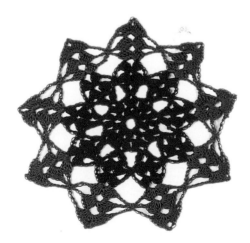

3

3 Green Shell Rounds

Rnd 6: Attach green thread with a sl st in center of any shell, ch 3, 3 dc in same sp, ch 7, *(4 dc, ch 3, 4 dc) in next shell, ch 7; repeat from * around, ending with 4 dc in same sp as beginning, ch 1, dc in top of beginning ch-3. {Nine (4 dc, ch 3, 4 dc) shells, 9 ch-7 arches}

Rnd 7: Ch 3, 4 dc in same sp, ch 6, skip ch-7 arch, *(5 dc, ch 3, 5 dc) shell in next shell, ch 6, skip ch-7 arch; repeat from * around, ending 5 dc in same sp as beginning, ch 1, dc in top of beginning ch-3. {Nine (5 dc, ch 3, 5 dc), 9 ch-6 arches}

Rnd 8: Ch 3, (3 dc, ch 1, dc) in same sp, *ch 4, working around chain arches from previous 2 rnds work sc, ch 4**, (dc, ch 1, 4 dc, ch 3, 4 dc, ch 1, dc) in next shell; repeat from * around ending at **, (dc, ch 1, 4 dc) in same sp as beginning, ch 3, sl st to join at top of beginning ch-3. Fasten off green thread.

4 Finishing

Weave in all ends securely, block with steam.

CHAPTER 14: Filet Crochet

Another traditional style of thread lace is filet crochet. Usually worked in rows, filet lace is characterized by its neat, geometric appearance. Simple or intricate designs are worked by making solid blocks of stitches interspersed between open, mesh squares. In traditional threadwork, there are several different common mesh sizes; these meshes are also used in contemporary filet work in yarn.

This chapter will introduce the specific type of chart used for filet, the arithmetic needed to plan a project, and offer options in both thread and yarn—a bookmark and a table topper. While filet crochet has traditionally been worked in very fine thread, many modern crocheters and designers prefer to use these designs with yarn. The demonstration photos show both; so choose what works best for your eyes and hands!

WHAT YOU'LL LEARN. . . . .

- How to make three different mesh sizes, in either yarn or thread
- How to determine the number of starting chains, depending on the chosen mesh dimension
- How to work solid and open blocks over each other

WHAT YOU'LL NEED . . . .

YARN OR THREAD

- 50 yds (46 m) of yarn or thread

HOOK

- Of appropriate size for chosen fiber (page 12)

NOTIONS

- Needle for weaving in ends

Filet Mesh Swatch

Mesh is the basis for all filet crochet. The size of the stitches used (either dc or tr) and the number of chains worked between stitches determines the size of each square in the mesh. Filet patterns are usually simply presented as charts, leaving the individual crocheter to decide on the mesh used. Different size meshes are appropriate for different projects, and it's really a matter of personal taste. A couple of factors that influence the decision are whether one tends to work tall-ish or short-ish dc stitches, and whether the picture being worked demands actual squares in the mesh or not. Another factor is whether the finished project should drape softly (as in an afghan or garment) or remain firm (as in a table mat or wall hanging). Let's start by working a small practice swatch of each type of mesh. Then we'll work some solid and some open blocks.

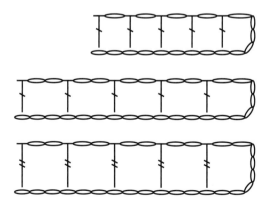

These symbol diagrams show one row of open blocks in each of the three common mesh sizes. Top: small mesh (dc, ch 1); center: medium mesh (dc, ch 2); bottom: large mesh (tr, ch 2).

As you begin to make the swatches, keep in mind that the goal is for the spaces between stitches to be as nearly square as possible. Depending on yarn or thread and hook choice, and on individual stitching style, some mesh styles may result in short-and-wide rectangles or in narrow-and-tall rectangles. When creating pictures from filet charts, rectangular blocks will distort the picture sometimes beyond recognition. It's a good idea at the start of every filet project to make some mesh swatches with the chosen fiber and choose the "right" mesh for making square squares!

1 Open Mesh Squares Beginning with Small Mesh

To make a small mesh swatch 5 squares wide (in older patterns, referred to as "5 meshes" wide), start with 14 ch. Why? Each square requires 2 ch (5 x 2 = 10), add 1 more for the top of the first square (10 + 1 = 11), add 3 for chain equivalent of first dc to start the row (11 + 3 = 14). Make the starting chains fairly loosely, whether using thread or yarn, as they will be worked in!

Row 1: Dc in 6th ch from hook (counts as ch 1, dc, ch 1), *ch1, skip 1 ch, dc in next ch; repeat from * across. Turn. Row 1 produces a little row of 5 boxes.

Row 2: Ch 4 (counts as dc, ch 1), dc in next dc, *ch 1, dc in next dc; repeat from * across, end with dc in 3rd ch of turning ch. Turn.

Row 3: Repeat Row 2. Do not fasten off.

2 Alternating Closed and Open Squares

Five squares of small mesh worked with #10 thread and #7 hook, and worsted yarn and G7 (4.5 mm) hook.

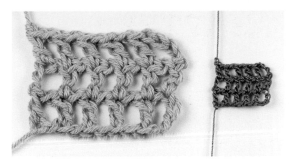

Three rows of "open squares" in small mesh.

TIP Make the chains loosely enough that each chain is as wide as the stitch tops on either side of it. This helps to keep the squares actually "square."

Next, let's alternate some "closed" or solid squares (also sometimes called "blocks") between the open squares. Here's the stitch symbol diagram for what we're about to do—although it's important to keep in mind that actual filet crochet patterns almost never include this type of diagram.

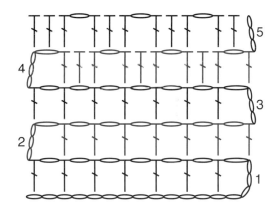

Row 4: Ch 4, sk next ch, *dc in next dc, dc in next ch (or in ch-1 sp), dc in next dc, ch 1, skip next ch; repeat from * across, end with dc in 3rd ch of turning ch. Turn.

Row 5: Ch 3, dc in next ch (or ch-1 sp), and dc in next dc, *ch 1, skip next st, dc in next dc, dc in next ch (or ch-1 sp), dc in next dc; repeat from * across working last dc in 3rd ch of turning ch. Turn.

(continued)

Troubleshooting

Work in the chain or in the chain space? When making a solid square over an open square, it's acceptable to work it either way. It's certainly easier to work in the chain space, and if the mesh squares have seemed a bit tall and thin (rectangular) this is a good way to "lower the ceiling" and make the enclosed space more of a true square. On the other hand, working in the space has a tendency to make the space less clean and clear as a square. If the dc stitches are on the short side, working in the space can almost make the space disappear! It's more difficult to work in the chain itself, but this will add height, keep the edges of the square good and straight and provide the most contrast between closed and open squares. The finished visual difference between the two is fairly subtle. In the end, you'll have to decide on the balance for yourself, between ease and precision, knowing that both are traditionally accepted ways of doing the stitch. Work Rows 4 and 5 one way, then repeat them using the other strategy, and decide which one is best for you. The choice may differ from project to project, depending on the yarn or thread and hook being used.

Filet Mesh Swatch (continued)

TIP When working in the chain, it's easier to get into it if the chin of the hook is used to pull down on the bottom bump of the chain, opening a space for the top of the hook to be inserted. LOOSE chains are also a huge help!

Make the same "5 square" swatch in medium and large meshes. The number of chains and the height of the stitches are different, but the logic of construction is the same. Here are stitch symbol diagrams to help in getting started:

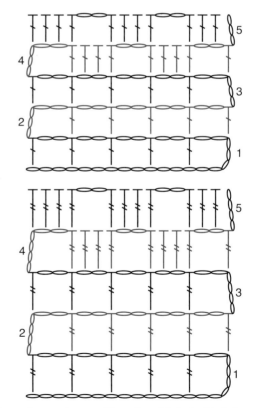

For medium mesh, start with 20 ch, and dc in the 8th ch from the hook. For large mesh, ch 21 and work the first tr in the 9th ch from the hook.

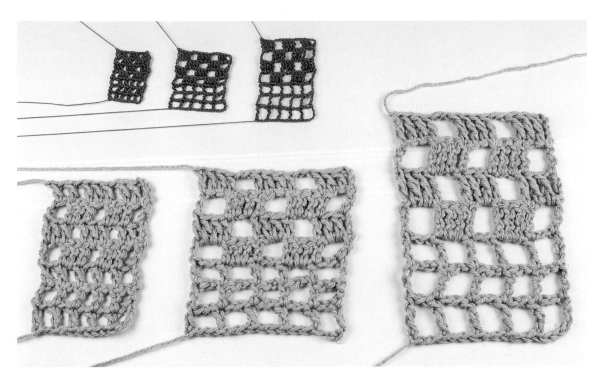

Compare swatches in small, medium, and large mesh in thread and in yarn.

WHAT YOU'LL LEARN . . . .

- How to read a filet chart in correct order and direction
- How to calculate the foundation chain for any filet chart

WHAT YOU'LL NEED . . . .

YARN

- 50 yds (46 m) or so of thread or smooth textured yarn

HOOK

- Of size appropriate to yarn/thread choice

NOTIONS

- 2 sticky notes for marking chart, one wide enough to cover a row of the chart, one much smaller to "flag" the beginning of the row
- Needle for weaving in ends

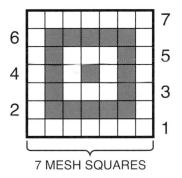

7 MESH SQUARES

Here's the chart for the practice swatch.

Reading Filet Crochet Charts

Unlike other styles of crochet, filet crochet patterns almost never give the same kind of row-by-row directions common to crochet. The projects are crocheted almost entirely from filet charts, and then pattern instructions detail any assembly and finishing steps needed. We'll start with a very simple chart, and gradually gain confidence in following filet charts, line by line!

(continued)

Reading Filet Crochet Charts (continued)

Like the familiar stitch symbol diagrams, a filet chart is read from the bottom up, with rows read in alternating directions. In this chart, the bottom row shows seven open mesh squares. Row 2 shows an open mesh square, followed by five solid squares/blocks, and then an open square/space again at the end. What the chart does NOT show is the number of individual stitches in any given row! This number is determined by the crocheter's choice of mesh size.

1 Foundation

Here's how to determine the length of the starting chain:

1. Determine the total number of squares, both open and solid in Row 1 of the chart—7 squares in our practice chart.

2. For small mesh, where a square consists of (ch 1, dc), multiply the number of squares by the two stitches it takes to make a square (7 × 2 = 14). For medium mesh, where a square is made of (ch 2, dc), it's three stitches to a square. (7 × 3 = 21). For large mesh, with a square consisting of (ch 2, tr), it's also three stitches to a square. (7 × 3 = 21).

3. Next add the extra chains needed for the turning chain at the beginning of the row—that's 3 for small and medium mesh and 4 for large mesh. So, our total now for small mesh is (14 + 3 = 17), medium mesh is (21 + 3 = 24), and large mesh with its taller stitches is (21 + 4 = 25).

4. Finally, we need the chains that will form the top of the first square if it's an open one as in this chart. For small mesh, add one more chain (17 + 1 = 18). For medium mesh starting with an open space, add two more chain (24 + 2 = 26). For large mesh, also add two more chain (25 + 2 = 27).

Make a note of the number of foundation chain needed for this chart in the chosen mesh: Small—18, Medium—26, Large—27.

TIP In future projects, where the first square may be a filled or solid one, omit #4 above—the total from #3 is the total for the foundation chain.

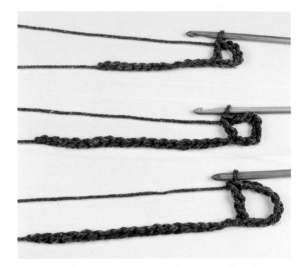

Foundation ch and first stitch. Top to bottom: small mesh, medium mesh, large mesh. For visibility, samples shown are worked in worsted yarn with G7 (4.50 mm) hook.

TIP Many crocheters find it helpful to use a sticky note to cover the chart above the current row, leaving visible the row being worked, and anything below it. In this way, it's easy to see what needs to be worked next, and whether it will be worked into a stitch or a space. Move the note up the chart as each new row is started. It may also be helpful to mark the side of the chart from which the current row begins. In symmetrical designs, such as this one, there's no harm in reading a row backwards. But if the chart contains any rows that are not right/left mirror images, correct direction of work across the chart becomes absolutely essential. Office supply aisles in department stores often carry pads of very small stickies, shaped as arrows, which are helpful for marking the row starts.

This chart has been masked and flagged with stickies, ready to work Row 3. Previous rows visible to make it easy to see what's being worked into, as the work progresses.

2 Read Row 1 from Right to Left

Having calculated the foundation chain, go ahead and start the first row. First determine where, in the foundation chain, the first dc or tr stitch should be placed. When working in small mesh, and an open space/blank square at the start, the first dc is made in the 6th ch from the hook. The 5 unworked chain form the top, bottom and ch-3 side of the first square. For medium mesh and an "open space" start, make the first dc in the 8th ch from the hook. For large mesh and an open space start, place the first tr in the 9th ch from the hook.

If the chart begins with a solid square or "block," small and medium mesh both start with dc in the 4th ch from the hook; large mesh starts with tr in the 5th ch from the hook.

Work across the row, just as in the previous swatch, making a total of 7 open squares or "spaces."

3 Complete the Chart

Continue to read even numbered rows from left to right and odd-numbered rows from right to left. Move the sticky markers up at the start of each row, shifting the smaller marker to note the direction of work for the current row. Since every row in this chart begins with an open space, there will always be 4 chain at the turn for small mesh, 5 for medium mesh, and 6 for large mesh. Count the turning chain as the first stitch and chain 1 or 2, and make the first stitch of the new row in the top of the next actual stitch of the previous row, skipping the chains at the top of the first square, just as in the first three rows of the previous practice swatch.

In other charts, where some or all rows begin with a solid square or "block," remember to chain only the normal turning chain for the stitch (dc or tr) in use. Make the second stitch immediately next to the turning chain, counting the turning chain as the fist stitch of the row, and as the right side edge of the first block of the chart.

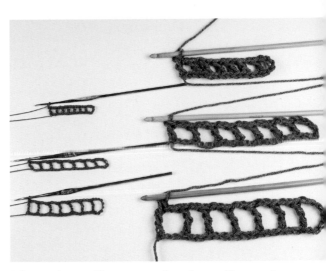

Left, top to bottom: Chart row 1, small, medium, and large mesh, worked in thread.

Right, top to bottom: Chart row 1, small, medium, and large mesh worked in worsted yarn.

Completed Swatches from practice chart. Note the variety achieved through yarn and mesh-size choices!

PROJECT 14: Filet Crochet Bookmark or Table Topper

The size and use of this project will be determined by choice of fiber. If thread is difficult to see and work with, choose a comfortable fiber for eyes and hands, and make the thicker, larger topper. If thread is not a problem at this point, make a delicate lace bookmark. While the samples show the bookmark made from the shamrock chart and topper made from the heart chart, they are interchangeable. The two charts could even be alternated within one project, if desired! Charts may always be interchanged if they contain the same number of mesh squares per row and same number of rows. They may also be worked in reverse, to create a mirror image, or from the side. Since each square on the chart represents a square made of stitches, the ability to turn a chart sideways enables the crocheter to create a variety of projects from a single chart.

WHAT YOU'LL LEARN . . . .

- How to make a whole project following filet charts—either bookmark in thread or topper in yarn
- How to make a decreased edge for a filet crochet project

WHAT YOU'LL NEED . . . .

YARN OR THREAD

- For bookmark: 150 yds (138 m) #10 cotton crochet thread
- For topper: smooth-textured cotton blend worsted-weight yarn
- Shown: Plymouth Yarns Jeannee Worsted (51% Cotton, 49% Acrylic, 50 g/110 yds), 1 skein main color, 2 skeins contrast color

HOOK

- For bookmark: steel size #7
- For centerpiece: size G7 (4.5 mm)

NOTIONS

- Needle to sew in yarn ends

(continued)

WHAT YOU'LL NEED . . . .

GAUGE

- In thread: 5 small mesh squares = 1″ (2.5 cm)
- In worsted yarn: 1 large mesh square = 1″ (2.5 cm)

FINISHED SIZES

- Bookmark: 12″ long × 3″ wide (30.5 × 7.5 cm)
- Centerpiece: 20 × 20″ (51 cm)

Other sizes will be obtained by using different sized thread, hook, or mesh

STITCHES AND ABBREVIATIONS USED

- chain = ch
- clip stitch = sl st
- double crochet = dc
- treble crochet = tr

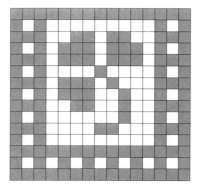 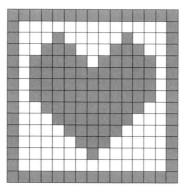 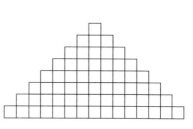

1 Plan the Project

First, decide whether thread or yarn is to be used. This decision determines the finished scale or size of the project, although the charts are the same size. Other sizes of thread may be used, and produce different sizes of finished projects. For example, if medium mesh is used for the bookmark, with #10 thread and a #7 hook, the piece will be around 5″ wide—wider than many people are accustomed to using for a bookmark. A smaller centerpiece can be made by using sport or fingering weight yarn instead of worsted, and/or by using a smaller mesh size. Delicate lace coasters can be made by following the directions for the centerpiece, but using small mesh, size 10 thread, and a #7 hook. It's easy to see that filet crochet offers tremendous versatility, but requires that decisions be made! For this project, choose a hook and fiber that are comfortable to see and work with. Make a small mesh swatch to see which mesh size suits, and use the process outlined in this chapter to determine the length of the starting chain.

TIP The reversed shamrock in the center of the bookmark demonstrates an important quality of filet crochet charts—they can be worked in any direction! To work in reverse (for any non-symmetrical shape) simply read the chart in reverse order, working odd-numbered rows from left to right and even rows from right to left. To work several repeats of a chart side by side, simply calculate a foundation chain long enough to accommodate the total number of mesh squares in the combined charts to be used. It's also possible to work a chart sideways, by turning the chart on its side, and counting the squares on what is now the base, to calculate the foundation chain. Then simply work the open squares and filled blocks of each row, allowing the picture to emerge from side to side instead of bottom to top.

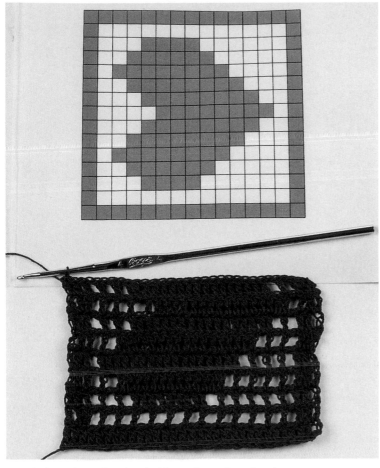

Here the heart chart is being worked from side to side, in thread.

In the case of the samples, both charts are 15 mesh squares wide, and both begin with a row of solid blocks rather than open mesh squares. Therefore, in small mesh (bookmark), begin with (15 × 2 = 30 + 3 = 33) 33 ch, and make the first dc in the 4th ch from the hook. Work across the row making a dc in each chain. The completed first row will consist of 31 dc, counting the turning chain as a stitch. For medium mesh, with the first row being solid blocks, (15 × 3 = 45 + 3 = 47) 47 chain make the foundation. In large mesh, as in the sample centerpiece, (15 × 3 = 45 +4 = 49) 49 ch make up the foundation. The first tr stitch will be worked in the 5th ch from the hook, followed by a tr in each ch across the row.

Next choose which chart to use—a bookmark with hearts or a green shamrock centerpiece would certainly work as well as the choices made for the samples. It would also work to use two shamrocks and a heart in the center of the bookmark, instead of the reversed shamrock!

From this point, directions will proceed assuming that the sample models are being followed; so adapt as necessary for any changes you've made in planning your own project.

(continued)

Foundation and first block for the bookmark and the centerpiece.

PROJECT 14: Filet Crochet Bookmark or Table Topper (continued)

2 Work the Main Chart

With the first row in place, simply proceed up the chart, as done in the practice. For the bookmark, when the chart is complete, start over again at Row 2. Row 15 and Row 1 of the chart are identical, and should not be duplicated between motifs.

For the bookmark, it may be desirable to reverse the direction of work for the center shamrock. If so, simply read each row in the opposite direction. For the centerpiece, fasten off when the main chart is complete, unless the edging will be worked in the same color. For the bookmark, work the main chart three times, and then do not fasten off, but turn in readiness for the first row of the edging.

3 Edging

When the main section of the project has been crocheted, work will continue along the top edge, following the edging chart. Notice that each row of the chart has fewer mesh squares than the row below it. This shaping will require a decrease at each end of each row. Work the first row, starting at the right hand edge of the top of the project. Make a turning chain of the height appropriate for the size mesh

In pattern language, the directions will often read, "slip stitch to end of first block." So, if working in small mesh, there will be three slip stitches—one in the stitch on the end, and one in each of the next two. If working in medium or large mesh, there will be four slip stitches.

being used, and complete the first solid block. When the row is finished, turn the work, but DO NOT CHAIN. Instead, work a slip stitch in the top of each stitch of the first solid block.

Now chain the appropriate number to begin the next row. Work Row 2 of the chart, ending with a stitch in the first stitch of the last block of Row 1. Again, turn, slip stitch across the first block, and then chain to begin the first block of Row 3. When the chart is complete, fasten off. The sample bookmark has the end edging only on the top, where it will hang out of the top of the book. If desired, the same edging can be worked along the bottom of the bookmark. Turn the work so that the original foundation chain is at the top, with the wrong side facing. Attach the thread in the stitch at the right hand corner, and proceed just as for the top edging.

For the centerpiece, the same edging process is worked for the top and bottom edges. Then the sides are edged. To edge the sides, turn the work so that the right side of the first row of the top edging is facing you, and an unworked side edge is at the top. Attach the yarn in the right hand corner stitch. Look at the row ends running along the top of the work. Each stitch represents one mesh square. So when working a solid block, evenly space the appropriate number of stitches across the length of that stitch, working into, rather than around the post of the stitch. When working an open square, place the first stitch at the beginning of a row end, make the appropriate number of chain, and then finish the block with a stitch where that row end joins the next. After the first row, the side edgings are worked exactly like the top and bottom edgings were. When each edging is finished, fasten off.

4 Finishing

Weave in all yarn or thread ends. The bookmark needs no further finishing. The centerpiece can be blocked, if desired, by following the yarn manufacturer's directions for washing and drying.

In the case of the sample, the yarn is machine washable and dryable, so it was washed, then dried in the dryer till almost dry. Then it was laid out flat with the corners pinned to prevent curling for the final drying.

Bonus Ideas

If you're comfortable working with steel hooks and thread, try making a set of coasters to match the table centerpiece. Work them exactly like the centerpiece, but on thread's smaller scale, using small mesh, in matching or coordinating colors.

Afghan squares can be made individually, using worsted yarn and small mesh. The squares can be made in a variety of colors, and then sewn or crocheted together. A simple Crab Stitch or Picot edging (see Chapter 11) will finish off the project.

CHAPTER 15:
Tunisian (or Afghan Stitch) Crochet

Tunisian crochet, (commonly called Afghan Stitch in the mid- to late- twentieth century), is a bit different from other crochet styles and traditions. It involves using a slightly different hook, and working all the stitches of a row at the same time, instead of completing each stitch before starting the next. Each row is worked in two "passes"—picking up a loop for each stitch on the first pass and then working the loops off and completing the stitches on the return pass. The fabric produced is somewhat thinner than fabric made with the same size hook and yarn in regular crochet. There are a large number of different stitches and textures possible in Tunisian crochet; this chapter will introduce the technique and the two most basic stitches. The project is a fun toddler's scarf with an extra surprise, using both stitches and simple shaping.

Getting Started with Tunisian—Practice Swatch

THE HOOK

Hooks for Tunisian crochet need a straight shaft (no thumb rest), and must be long enough to accommodate all the stitches of a row, like a knitting needle. Several styles are available.

Because all the stitches of a row are held on the hook at once, Tunisian crochet is generally worked with either a longer hook, or a hook with a cable attached to its end. For small projects, with only short rows, a regular crochet hook with a straight shaft will work just fine. A rubber band can be placed around the far end of the hook to keep stitches from sliding off, if necessary. Proper gauge requires the use of a straight shaft, though. Ergonomic handles and thumb rests will get in the way of the loops on the shaft of the hook. Cabled hooks are great for very large projects, because the cable allows the weight of the project to rest in the crocheter's lap, instead of being lifted for every single stitch.

To create a fabric with great drape and texture, most contemporary Tunisian patterns call for a hook somewhat larger than would be used for regular crochet with a given yarn. The example pictures show worsted-weight yarn with a size L (8 mm) hook, to allow visibility; however, in the project, we'll be using a J or K (6 to 7 mm) hook with worsted yarn. The swatches and project in this chapter all have short enough rows that a special Tunisian or Afghan hook is not required.

THE TECHNIQUE— FOUNDATION AND FIRST FORWARD PASS

Start with a chain, as in any regular crochet. For the first practice swatch, start with 16 ch. Locate the "bottom bumps" of the chain just made (See page 18). Insert the hook under the bottom bump of the 2nd ch from the hook, yo and draw up a loop (2 loops on hook). Next, insert the hook under the bottom bump of the next ch, yo and draw up a loop (3 loops on hook). Continue across the row, picking up a loop in this manner in each ch. At the end, there will be 16 loops on the hook—one for each of the 15 stitches, and one that was on the hook at the start.

FIRST RETURN PASS

Now here's one of the differences between Tunisian and regular crochet: the turning chain is done between the forward and reverse passes of each row, rather than at the start of a row. So, with all 16 loops on the hook, yo and pull through one loop (turning chain made)

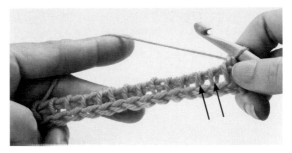

The first row of Tunisian crochet, completed. Most Tunisian stitch patterns begin with this same first or foundation row. Note the vertical strands of yarn, marked with arrows. Each stitch has one of these "vertical bars" and they become very important in following rows.

Now, we'll finish each stitch, by "working them off the hook." Yo and pull through 2 loops; there are now 15 loops on the hook. Yo and pull through 2 again, leaving 14 on the hook. Repeat this motion all the way across the row, until only one loop remains on the hook. The work is not turned, and all rows are worked with the right side facing.

FORWARD AND REVERSE PASSES FOR TUNISIAN SIMPLE STITCH (TSS)

The forward pass of the second row is where our two Tunisian stitches differ from one another. It's all in the insertion of the hook. For Tunisian Simple Stitch, abbreviated tss, we will insert the hook under the front vertical bar of each stitch.

Forward Pass: Continue across the row, inserting the hook under each front vertical bar, in turn, and drawing up a loop, thus loading the hook for the row. There will again be 16 loops on the hook at the end of the forward pass. Many beginners find

Skipping the vertical bar immediately below the hook's shaft, insert the hook under the next front vertical bar. Yo and draw up a loop.

it a bit tricky to locate the point of insertion for the last stitch in the forward pass. In order to create a finished edge and maintain correct stitch count from row to row, the final insertion is under two strands, instead of one. At the last stitch, insert the hook under the two strands of yarn at the far left edge of the previous row. This creates a braided edge, identical in appearance to the other edges of the fabric.

Reverse Pass: As in the first row, begin the reverse pass with a ch-1 (yo and pull through 1 loop). Now work across the row, repeating the (yo and pull through 2 loops) sequence. The completed second row appears to have a gap of holes; don't worry. This is normal, and each row, as the forward pass is worked, compacts the previous row, filling the holes.

The fabric will also begin to curl forward from the bottom edge; this is also normal. Curling is most pronounced if the hook is small in comparison to the yarn, and if loops are not pulled through all the way to the top of the work; but a certain amount of curling is inevitable, and will be sorted out in finishing steps for any project.

Work several more rows, being conscious to locate the final two strands for insertion in the last stitch of each forward pass. It's also important to keep the very first loop, on the hook at the start of the forward pass, a bit snug, and to work the "chain one" between the passes a little loosely. This combination will create smooth edges. If the right edge is a bit ruffly, or the left edge a bit tight, pay careful attention to snugging the beginning loop and to making the chain between passes a nice, loose one.

BINDING OFF

When any piece of Tunisian crochet is completed, a final step is needed. This "bind-off" compresses the last row of actual stitches, so that they match the rest of the fabric. It also moves the work across to the left edge of the piece, where any normal last stitch of regular crochet would end.

To bind off, insert the hook as usual for a forward pass, but complete a slip stitch by pulling the loop through the one already on the hook. The first stitch is now "bound off," and there is still only one loop on the hook. Insert the hook under the next front vertical bar and complete a slip stitch, again leaving one loop on the hook. Work across the row until all 15 stitches are bound off.

The neat square boxes that appear on the right side of Tunisian simple stitch are often used as a background for counted cross-stitch embroidery. This particular combination was very popular in several previous generations, and is revived from time to time in contemporary designs.

On the left, a 6-row swatch of Tunisian Simple Stitch that has not been bound off. Note the spaces in the top row. On the right, a 6-row swatch of tss that has been properly bound off. The top row has no appearance of "holeyness." All four edges of the swatch have identical braided edges. The piece is fastened off in normal crochet manner.

Tunisian Knit Stitch (tks)

The second most common and basic Tunisian stitch is Tunisian Knit Stitch, abbreviated tks. It begins with a foundation row exactly like the foundation row for tss, above. So make a chain of 16, and work the forward and reverse passes of the foundation row as in the tss swatch.

FORWARD PASS—A DIFFERENT INSERTION

Again ignoring the front vertical bar directly below the hook, for tks insert the hook between the front and back vertical bars (refer to illustration above), all the way to the back of the work, as in regular crochet. Yo and draw up a loop to the front and top of the work. Proceed to the next stitch, inserting between front and back vertical bars and drawing up a loop. Continue across the row in this manner.

The insertion for the last stitch of the row is the same as it was for tss—under the two leftmost strands at the edge of the work. As before, work a chain stitch and then proceed with the reverse pass, working (yo and pull through 2 loops) for each stitch across until only one loop remains on the hook. It's here, with Row 2 completed, that the difference in texture of the fabric becomes very obvious!

Work several more rows, becoming comfortable with the stitch, and then bind off. Insertion for binding off is in the same spot as for the main rows of the stitch. This stitch looks better when bound off using single crochet instead of slip stitch. Insert the hook between the two vertical bars, yo

Loops drawn up in forward pass for tks.

Tunisian Knit Stitch is so named because the right side of the fabric mimics the appearance of knitted Stockinette stitch. The fabric is thicker, however, than a knitted fabric.

and draw up a loop, and then complete as a single crochet: yo and pull through 2 loops, leaving 1 loop on the hook. Continue in the same manner across the row and fasten off as usual. As with tss, the fabric has a tendency to curl up from the bottom edge; blocking, seaming and edging in a project will help it to lie flat.

TIP Binding off for Tunisian crochet can be done with any regular crochet stitch. Sometimes a pattern will specify one stitch or another to use for binding off. Follow those instructions when given; but when not specified, bind off with slip stitch for tss and with sc for tks.

Right swatch is unblocked; Left swatch has been blocked to reduce curl.

PROJECT 15:
Snuggly Scarf with Pocket Pal

Cushiony Tunisian stitching, bright colors, and the surprise pal in the pocket all combine to make this winter warmer a hit with small children. The scarf can be worked wider and longer for a larger person, but the comfort of a small, quiet toy in the pocket is a special treat for youngsters. The pocket can also be used to keep mittens or gloves from getting lost! The recommended yarn is a very soft, squishy, washable wool. However, any worsted yarn will work for the project.

WHAT YOU'LL LEARN . . . .

- How to make a small stuffed toy using Tunisian simple stitch

- How to use decreases for shaping in Tunisian simple stitch

- How to make a scarf with pocket using Tunisian knit stitch

WHAT YOU'LL NEED . . . .

YARN

- Worsted weight

- Shown: Plymouth Yarns Select Merino Worsted (100% Superwash Fine Merino Wool; 100 g/218 yds), 1 skein blue #6 (A), ½ skein red #37 (B), ½ skein gold #38 (C), small amount brown #29 (D)

HOOKS

- Straight shafted regular crochet hooks, or "afghan" hooks in sizes H (5 mm) (for pet) and J (6 mm) (for scarf)

NOTIONS

- Large-eyed yarn needle

- 4 sewing pins

- Small amount of wool or fiberfill stuffing

FINISHED SIZE

- 4" wide by 36" long (10 × 91.5 cm) , including looped fringe. Pet is 3¼" wide by 5" tall (8.5 × 12.5 cm), including feet

GAUGE

- With smaller hook working in Tunisian simple stitch, 9 sts and 9 rows = 2" (5 cm)

- With larger hook working in Tunisian knit stitch, 8 sts and 8 rows = 2" (5 cm). Exact gauge is not essential to this project

STITCHES AND ABBREVIATIONS USED

- chain = ch

- single crochet = sc

- slip stitch = sl st

- tunisian knit stitch = tks

- tunisian simple stitch = tss

- stitch(es) = st(s)

- yarn over = yo

1 Make Scarf, Starting with the Pocket

With larger hook and B, ch 15.

Row 1: Work forward and reverse passes of tks. {14 sts}

Rows 2–17: Repeat Row 1.

Bind off with a row of sc. Fasten off. Turn work.

Row 18: With wrong side of work facing and A insert hook in each stitch of bind-off row, and draw up a loop in each. Work reverse pass.

Row 19: Work forward and reverse passes of tks. {14 sts}

Repeat Row 19 until A section measures 34" long.
Bind off with sl st. Fasten off.

2 Scarf Edging and Assembly

Fold scarf at join between pocket and main sections, so that right side of each piece is facing. Pin in place, so edge stitches match.

Rnd 1: With right side facing, attach B with a sc in last stitch of bind-off at opposite end of work from pinned section, work 1 sc in each row end of Tks, until folded section is reached. Now working through both loops both pieces together and keeping stitches matched, continue to work sc. At corner, work 3 sc in first row end,

then work 1 sc in each stitch of Pocket bind-off. At corner, work 3 sc in first row end. Continue up long side, working sc through both thicknesses of pocket section, then 1 sc in each row end of scarf. At corner, work 3 sc in last row end, then work across stitches of bind-off. Join with a sl st to first sc worked in this round. Fasten off.

3 Looped Fringe

Row 1: With right side facing and larger hook, attach A to B

pocket end with a sl st in right hand side of B bind-off (where red and blue scarf sections join at folded crease). *Ch 12, sc in next st; repeat from * across. Fasten off.

Row 2: At opposite end of scarf, attach B with a sc in right hand side of A bind-off; *ch 12, sc in next st; repeat from * across. Fasten off. Weave in all yarn ends securely. Center front edge of pocket curls outward—this is intentional and allows the stuffed toy to peek out of the pocket!

Row 1: Pick up a loop in back bump of each ch for forward pass. Work reverse pass across row {10 sts}

Rows 2–29: Work forward and reverse passes of tss. Piece should measure 8" long. Work extra rows or fewer rows if necessary to achieve correct measurement.

Bind off with a row of sl st; do NOT fasten off.

5 Assemble Toy Main Section

Fold the work in half, so Row 1 meets bind-off row. Working through both pieces and matching sts, sc in each row end to fold. At fold, work 2 sc, then work 1 sc in each st across folded edge, inserting hook under vertical bar of each st.

Work 2 sc in last st at left end, then sc through both thicknesses working in each st from fold to open short end. Fasten off leaving 36" of tail. RS of edging is front of Pet. Stuff lightly with wool batting or fiberfill, then use 36" tail to work sc through both pieces, matching sts of Rows 1 and 29, to complete closing with bottom seam. Join last st to first st of edging with a sl st. Fasten off and weave in ends.

(continued)

4 Crochet Toy Main Section

The head and body of the "Pet" are worked as one long rectangle, which is then folded in half. Seams will be created from a sc edging, and arms and legs are then worked on by picking up loops for stitches at the appropriate places.

Starting with smaller hook and C, ch 11.

6

6 Make the Legs/Feet

Both the legs and arms of the little creature are shaped by using decreases. To decrease in Tunisian simple stitch, the hook is inserted under the vertical bars of two adjacent stitches at the same time, combining those two stitches into one when the reverse pass is worked.

Row 1: Forward pass: With front side facing, begin at right corner of bottom seam; with smaller hook and D, pick up a loop in each of 6 sts from corner working toward center. Work reverse pass.

Row 2: Forward pass: Insert hook under vertical bar of both first and 2nd sts together.

Row 2 continued: Yo and draw up a loop, insert hook under vertical bar of next st and draw up a loop, insert hook under bars of next 2 sts together and draw up a loop, insert hook under vertical bar of last stitch and draw up a loop. {5 loops on hook}. Work reverse pass. Two decreases have been worked in this row, and 4 sts now remain.

Row 3: Forward pass: Decrease 1 st over first 2 sts as in previous row, pick up 1 loop in each remaining st. {4 loops on hook}. Work reverse pass. {3 sts}

Rows 4 and 5: Work even (no further decreases) over 3 sts.

Bind off with a row of sl st. Fasten off leaving 8" of tail. Fold Row 5 up over Row 4 and sew, working through bind off and Row 3.

Second Leg

Row 1: Forward pass: With front of pet facing, finished leg at the right, smaller hook and D, pick up a loop in each of 6 sts to edge. Work reverse pass. {6 sts}

Row 2: Repeat Row 2, forward and reverse passes, of first leg. {4 sts}.

Row 3: Forward pass: Insert hook under vertical bar of first st and draw up a loop, decrease over next 2 sts, draw up a loop in last st. {4 loops on hook}. Work reverse pass. {3 sts}

Rows 4 and 5: Repeat Rows 4 and 5 of first leg.

Repeat bind off of first leg. Fold and sew as first leg. Fasten off. Weave in tails of both legs.

7 Left Arm

The arms are worked as separate steps, because their shaping requires a different order of decreases, to create a mirror image, with both arms having the same final appearance.

Row 1: Forward pass: Starting just above left leg, with front of Pet facing, smaller hook and D, skip 3 sts of side edge. Pick up a loop in next st and each of next 4 sts. {6 loops on hook}. Work reverse pass. {5 sts}

Row 2: Forward pass: Decrease over first 2 sts, pick up one loop in each remaining st across. {5 loops on hook}. Work reverse pass. {4 sts}

Rows 3 and 4: Repeat Row 2, working 3 sts and 2 sts respectively.

Row 5: Forward pass: Pick up one loop in each st. Reverse pass: Yo and pull through all 3 loops on hook. Fasten off.

The completed Left Arm has a straight upper edge and a slanted lower edge, where the decreases were worked.

8 Right Arm

Row 1: Forward pass: With front side of pet facing, smaller hook and D, pick up a loop in side edging st directly across body from top of completed left arm. Pick up a loop in each of next 4 sts. {6 loops on hook}. Work reverse pass. {5 sts}

Row 2: Forward pass: Insert hook under vertical bar of each stitch and draw up a loop. Reverse pass: (here is another method of decreasing in Tunisian crochet) ch 1, yo and pull through 3 loops (reverse pass decrease made), *yo and pull through 2 loops; repeat from * across. {4 sts}

Row 3: Forward pass: Insert hook under vertical bar of each stitch and draw up a loop. Reverse pass: Repeat reverse pass of Row 2. {3 sts}

Row 4: Forward pass: Insert hook under vertical bar of each stitch and draw up a loop. Reverse pass: Repeat reverse pass of Row 2. {2 sts}

Row 5: Forward pass: Insert under vertical bars of both remaining stitches together and draw up a loop. Reverse pass: Yo and pull through all 3 loops on hook. Fasten off. Weave in yarn tails of both arms.

9 Facial Features

With D, sew a diagonal line across each top corner of head, to form ears. Use scraps of A and B to embroider a simple face, with nose centered in row just above tops of arms.

Yarn tails from embroidered face and ears can be hidden inside stuffing for invisibility. Alternatively, "safety eyes" can be attached according to manufacturer's instructions, in 6th row from top of head, before stuffing.

CHAPTER 16: Tips, Tricks, and Shortcuts to Success

Having mastered the basics and explored some of the traditional techniques, all that remains to gain is experience ... and a few little tricks that make crochet faster, easier, and the results more polished in final appearance. The three "little tricks" in this chapter will work wonders in adding to your confidence as an intermediate-level crocheter. Instead of starting every project with a chain, this chapter will introduce the "Magic Ring" or adjustable loop (for work in the round) and the "chainless" foundation stitches (for work in rows). You'll also learn how to turn rows of dc without a turning chain—working an actual stitch at the start of each row. We'll use these new skills to make a chic hooded scarf in a bold combination of colors and chunky yarn.

WHAT YOU'LL LEARN . . . .

- How to start work in the round with an adjustable ring
- How to close and finish the ring securely
- How to make a crocheted button

WHAT YOU'LL NEED . . . .

YARN

- Approx. 10 yds (9.2 m) of worsted or chunky yarn

HOOK

- Since a button needs a stiff finished texture, use a hook 1 to 2 sizes smaller than would be used for a softer fabric in the chosen yarn. The sample photos show chunky (#5) yarn with an H (5 mm) hook. If using worsted (#4) yarn, choose an F or G (3.75 or 4.25 mm).

NOTIONS

- Large-eyed yarn needle
- One stitch marker

Crocheted Buttons Using the "Magic" Adjustable Ring

When starting a project in the round, we have previously worked a short chain, slip stitched the ends to make a ring, and then worked into the ring for the first round of the motif or hat. This is a fine way, the traditional way, to begin work in the round ... but recently some ingenious crocheter discovered that it's possible to start with a simpler process, and make a hole that closes completely and tightly when finished! Working into the adjustable ring is as easy as working a row of stitches straight, and the "magic" happens when the tail is pulled and the ring closes up. The technique is called by a variety of names: "magic circle," "magic ring," "adjustable loop," "adjustable ring," but they all refer to the same process. Whether specified in the pattern or not, this technique can be substituted for the chain/slip stitch ring at the start of any design that does not need an open "donut hole" at its center when complete. It can be used in any of the hat, motif, or flower patterns in the previous chapters. However, the doily pattern in Chapter 13 would not be a good place to use an adjustable ring start, because the finished design does have an open hole at its center. We'll use the adjustable ring to create buttons for this chapter's project.

1 Make the Loop

Leaving a 4 to 6" (10 to 15 cm) tail, loop the yarn once around an index finger, so that the tail end is closer to you than the yarn ball end.

Remove the loop from the finger, and pinch to hold it.

While holding the ring, insert the hook into the ring, reaching under the front (tail end) strand, catch the back strand in the hook, and (while still pinching the loop together) pull that strand through to the front.

Yarn over and pull through the loop on the hook.

2 Work in the Loop

The loop is now made and the first chain of the turning chain to begin the first round is complete. If substituting the adjustable ring for a chain loop start, you can now start reading the pattern at the point where it directs the first round. If sc is to be worked in the ring, there are no additional chains needed; simply insert the hook into the big ring and work the directed number (usually 6) of sc in the ring, as if it were a chain loop. Yes, it's large and looks funny . . . but Step 3 will "magically" take care of that! If the pattern calls for dc stitches, then two more chain are needed at this point, to start the round. For the purpose of our buttons, start with 6 sc in the ring. Many contemporary patterns simply state the number of stitches in a ring, and leave it up to the crocheter whether to start with the traditional ring of joined chain, or with the adjustable ring. Working the stitches in the ring, make sure to work around both strands (ring and tail) for every stitch. This is very important for the next step.

Working 6 sc in the ring.

(continued)

3 Close the Ring

Depending on the yarn's texture and fiber content, the ring may loosen up somewhat as the first couple of rounds in a larger project (such as a hat or large motif) are worked. Don't worry; simply pull the tail again. When a couple of rounds are complete, the tail can be threaded onto a yarn needle and woven in, as usual. In the present case, where we are making a small button, and will use the tail to attach the button to the project, simply ignore any loosening, and when the button is nearly complete, pull the tail again to tighten it down.

4 Complete the Button

Place a marker in the top of the first sc made. Now work in spiral, moving the marker to the first stitch of each following round.

Rnd 2: Work 2 sc in each stitch around. {12 sc}

Rnd 3: Sc in blo of each stitch around. {12 sc in blo}

Rnd 4: Sc2tog (decrease) 6 times, working through blo in each st, slip stitch to join last st to first st of rnd. Fasten off, leaving a 6-8" tail. Pull both tails firmly to the Rnd 4 side of the work. {6 sts}

Now here's the "magic": Pull the tail firmly.

Rounds 1–3 completed.

If all the stitches were correctly worked so that both strands of the ring are included in the base of each stitch, pulling the tail will magically close the ring, pulling the bases of all 6 stitches together tightly.

Completed button—use the two tails for attaching to the project.

Troubleshooting

If the ring won't close, check to make sure that every stitch was worked into the actual center of the ring, enclosing both strands of the adjustable ring in the base of every stitch.

(Almost) Chainless Foundation Stitches

Many crocheters shy away from patterns that have a long starting edge, because the idea of making a chain that long and then working a long row into the chain, is just overwhelming. Many crocheters really struggle with making the two edges of the project at the same tension—that chained edge just seems to come out loose and ruffly or tight and stiff. And then there are projects such as socks and top-down sweaters, where it's really desirable to have a stretchy neckline or cuff—and a chained edge has NO stretch. In response to these challenges, another starting technique has become popular in the first decade of the 21st century. It's sometimes called "chain-free" or "chainless," but the truth is, there is still a very small chain—roughly equal to the turning chain for the stitch being used. So, a project with a long row of dc at its base will start with 3 ch, rather than as many as 200–300! The actual stitches used for this method of starting are called "foundation stitches," because each stitch comprises both a single chain and the stitch worked into it, in a single unit attached to the foundation unit before and after it. The abbreviation for foundation single crochet is fsc. For foundation double crochet the abbreviation is fdc. There are also foundation stitches for starting with half-double crochet or trebles. They are designated the same way, by adding the letter "f" to the beginning of the regular stitch abbreviation. They are made by the same basic method. In this chapter, we'll learn fsc and fdc, and then use both of them in the project.

WHAT YOU'LL LEARN. . . . .

- How to make foundation single crochet (fsc) and foundation double crochet (fdc) stitches.
- How (and when) to substitute foundation stitches for a chained beginning in project patterns

WHAT YOU'LL NEED . . . .

YARN

- Worsted (#4) weight, approx. 20 yds (18.5 m)

HOOK

- Size J (6 mm)

NOTION

- One stitch marker

1 Foundation Single Crochet, First Stitch

In all the foundation stitches, the first stitch of the project is different than all the following stitches, as it does actually begin with a chain. After the first stitch, all following stitches are identical to one another. The chain at the beginning of the first stitch in fsc does not count as a stitch.

The first stitch is now complete. Directly below the hook is the top of the sc. The "chain" is the loop with the marker.

Ch 2 and insert the hook in the "bottom bump" of the first ch made (2nd from the hook), yo and draw up a loop.

Yo and pull through 1 loop, leaving 2 loops on hook. Place marker in the chain thus created, just below the hook.

(continued)

Yo and pull through both loops on hook.

2 Second and Following Stitches

Insert the hook under both strands of the marked "chain" loop, yo and draw up a loop.

Yo and pull through 1 loop, move marker to adjacent loop to the right (loop that just came off the hook). This is the new "chain."

TIP When "drawing up a loop" to start each new fsc, pull that loop through a little farther than usual. This helps in two ways: it makes the "chain" the same size as the top of the stitch being created, evening tension for the row; and it makes the "chain" easier to see for the start of the next stitch.

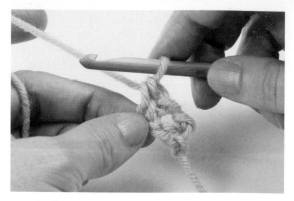

Yo and pull through 2 loops, second stitch is complete. Repeat this step as many times as directed. If the pattern states 10 fsc, then work through the steps for the first stitch, the second stitch and 8 more repeats of the second stitch. Use the marker as long as necessary, until it's easy to see the "chain" part of the stitch, where the hook will be inserted to begin the next stitch. The marker is not necessary once you're reading the stitches comfortably.

10 fsc completed. Stitches are counted from the loop immediately below the hook, which is the top of the most recent stitch completed, although it feels like the row is being worked "upside down" as each stitch is in progress.

Just for comparison, take a moment and make a chain of 11, then work 1 sc in 2nd ch from hook and sc in each ch across. Compare the two 10-stitch starts. It should be easy to notice the difference in stretch! Working fsc takes a little longer than chains, but MUCH less time (once the process is familiar) than making a large number of sc into a chain! In addition to being a great way to start projects or pieces that have a solid row of sc at the beginning, a row of fsc can also serve as a very nice drawstring.

SUBSTITUTING FSC IN PATTERNS

When substituting a row of fsc for a chain, turning chain and row of sc, remember to make one fewer stitch than the pattern's beginning chain—the turning chain was worked as part of the first fsc stitch. (This is the reason that the first stitch is different than all the rest. It begins with its own "chain" base, and the turning chain for the row of sc being simultaneously created.) At the end of the fsc row, turn the work and begin reading the pattern with the turning chain to start the pattern's Row 2.

FOUNDATION DOUBLE CROCHET (FDC) FIRST STITCH

This stitch is made in a very similar way to the fsc. But we'll start with 3 ch, and yarn over before inserting the hook in the bottom bump of the first chain made.

Just as before, yo and draw up a loop, yo and pull through 1, and mark the completed "chain." Now (yo and pull through 2 loops) twice, to complete the double crochet.

Completed first fdc stitch.

Yo before beginning each following stitch, insert the hook into the marked "chain" and draw up a loop, yo and pull through 1 to make the new "chain," and complete the dc. Here's a row of 10 completed fdc. As usual, on the front or right side, the top loop of each stitch is slightly offset to the right of the stitch's post.

It's optional whether to count the beginning chain at the far right of the row as a stitch or not, a matter of personal choice. The author frequently decides differently from project to project, depending on appearance. If counting the beginning chain, then the photo above actually shows a starting row of 11 stitches. Keep in mind the choice you've made about that beginning chain, when deciding how many fdc to make to actually start a project. In the project for this chapter, it's assumed that the beginning chain will not count as a stitch, since the ends of the row will be incorporated into a seam.

TIP Just as when beginning with chains, if working a very long row of stitches, counting is easier when markers are placed at regular intervals. Foundation stitches are not quite as easy as chains to "undo" at the end if extras are made and then the following row worked.

SUBSTITUTING FDC IN PATTERNS

When a project pattern begins with a chain and then a row of dc, remember that the last 3 chain made form the turning chain, which stands in place of the first dc of the row. So, when substituting fdc for the chain, make 2 fewer fdc than the number of chain called for. If the pattern provides stitch counts, look at the count for completed Row 1. This is another way to determine the number of fdc to make.

Yo with both strands of the LOOP, still holding fast. This can be done by simply moving the hook to the back, under the excess of extended loop. Still holding the loop on the hook, insert the tip of the hook in the first stitch of the row.

Chainless Dc Turns

This technique requires some practice to get "just right," but when mastered, completely eliminates the turning chain in rows that begin with a double crochet stitch.

Yo and draw up a loop, still holding the first loop steady in place on the hook.

STEP 1

Begin with a foundation row of 10 fdc already worked (or work 12 ch, dc in 4th ch from hook and each ch across. {10 dc})

Work several rows, making chainless turns, till the technique becomes familiar and comfortable. Now you're ready to put all these "tricks" to use in the Harlequin Shells Hooded Scarf.

Yo and pull through both the first loop and the double-strand of the second loop on the hook. Now the finger holding the original loop can let go.

Turn the work to start the second row, and extend the loop on the hook to approximately the height of a row of dc. Place a finger to hold the loop on the hook. It is absolutely essential that this finger hold the loop tightly through the next 2 steps—DON'T LET GO!

Complete the stitch: Yo and pull through the two loops on the hook. Place a marker in both strands of the loop just beneath the hook. It's the top of this stitch, but can be a little difficult to recognize when coming back in the following row, searching for the correct location for that row's last stitch. Marking makes it visible.

PROJECT 16:
Harlequin Shells Hooded Scarf

In bulky single-ply, "roving" style yarn, this ultra warm hooded scarf works up quickly. A simple stitch pattern of staggered shells in contrasting colors makes a geometric visual statement, and the optional tassel adds a touch of whimsy. Winter winds hold no menace to a woman wrapped in this hood and generous scarf!

WHAT YOU'LL LEARN . . . .

- How to use foundation stitches to extend a row
- How to use a crocheted button in the context of a chunky hooded scarf
- How to make a tassel

WHAT YOU'LL NEED . . . .

YARN

- Bulky (#5) single ply or "roving" style yarn
- Shown: Valley Yarns Berkshire Bulky (WEBS) (85% Wool/15% Alpaca, 100 g/108 yds), 2 balls #42 Dark Gray Heather (A), 1 ball # 41 Light Gray Heather (B), 1 ball #07 Black (C), 1 ball #15 Red (D)

HOOKS

- 10 mm (hooks this large are called by various letter names by different manufacturers; it's the actual measurement that affects gauge, however)
- H (5 mm) for button

NOTIONS

- Large-eyed yarn needle
- 2 stitch markers
- 5½" × 7½" (14 × 18 cm) piece of sturdy cardboard OR DVD movie case
- Large scissors (at least 4" (10 cm) blades)

FINISHED SIZE

- One size fits all. Hood is 12½" high by 10½" (32 × 27 cm) front edge to back seam. Scarf is 86" long by 7" wide (218.5 × 18 cm)

GAUGE

- With larger hook, 4 foundation double crochet (fdc) = 2" (5 cm). Exact gauge is not necessary for this project, but significant gauge difference will affect finished size

(continued)

WHAT YOU'LL NEED . . . .

STITCHES AND ABBREVIATIONS USED

- chain = ch
- slip stitch = sl st
- foundation double crochet = fdc
- foundation single crochet = fsc
- single crochet = sc
- double crochet = dc

- right side = RS
- wrong side = WS
- solid shell = s-shell—5 dc worked in same stitch or space
- lace shell = (dc, ch 1, dc, ch 1, dc) all in same stitch or space
- stitch(es) = st(s)

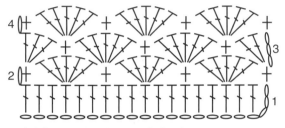

Symbol diagram of stitch pattern for hood.

1 Start Hood at Front Edge

Row 1 (RS): With larger hook and A, fdc 55. Turn.

Row 2: Ch 1, sc in first st, *sk next 2 sts, s-shell in next st, sk next 2 sts, sc in next st; repeat from * across. Fasten off. Turn. Place a stitch marker in the end stitch at each end of this row. These markers will be used later for scarf stitch placement. {9 shells}

Row 3: Attach B with a dc in first st, work 2 more dc in same st (half-shell made), skip next 2 sts, sc in next st, *skip next 2 sts, s-shell in next sc, skip next 2 sts, sc in next st; repeat from * across to last 3 sts, skip next 2 sts, 3 dc in last sc of row. Fasten off. Turn. {8 shells, 2 half-shells}

Row 4: Attach C with a sc in first st, *skip next 2 sts, s-shell in next sc, skip next 2 sts, sc in next st; repeat from * across. Fasten off. Turn. {9 shells}

Row 5: With D, work same as Row 3. Fasten off. Turn.

Row 6: With C, work same as Row 4. Fasten off. Turn.

Row 7: With B, work same as Row 3. Fasten off. Turn.

Row 8: With A, work same as Row 4. Do NOT fasten off. Turn.

Row 9: Chainless dc turning st in first st (or ch 3 and count as st), work 2 more dc in same st, complete row same as Row 3. Turn. Do NOT fasten off.

Row 10: Repeat Row 2, but do not fasten off. Turn.

Row 11: Repeat Row 9, and do not fasten off. Turn.

Row 12: Repeat Row 10. Fasten off, leaving 24" or so tail for sewing seam.

2 Sew Hood Back Seam

Fold Row 12 in half with right side facing out. (Right side of the hood is right side of Row 1 and all odd-numbered rows). Thread yarn tail onto large-eyed yarn needle and whip stitch a seam, working through 1 loop of each thickness, matching stitches, from edge to center of Row 12. Leave any excess tail for attaching tassel in finishing step.

(continued)

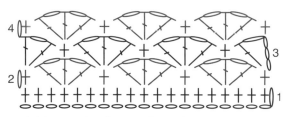

Symbol diagram of stitch pattern for scarf.

3 Make Scarf, Attached

Row 1: With larger hook and A, fsc 75, hold hood with WS facing and sc in marked st at one end of hood Row 2, working in ends of rows across edge evenly space 39 sc across hood, ending at marker on other end of hood Row 2, fsc 75. {189 sc}

TIP To begin an fsc extension when there are already stitches in the row, start by inserting the hook under the front legs of the last crochet stitch made, similar to when closing a picot (see Chapter 11 if necessary, to review the picot and the parts of the crochet stitch). Complete the fsc like a second or following fsc stitch, NOT like the first one when starting a new project.

Row 2: Ch 1, sc in each of first 2 sts, skip next 2 sts, l-shell in next st, skip next 2 sts, *sc in next st, skip next 2 sts, l-shell in next st, skip next 2 sts; repeat from * across to last 2 sts, sc in each of last 2 sts. Fasten off. Turn. {31 l-shells}

Row 3: Attach B with a dc in first st, (dc, ch 1, dc) in next st, skip next 2 sts, sc in next st, skip next 2 sts, *l-shell in next sc, skip next 2 sts, sc in next st, skip next 2 sts; repeat from * across to last 2 sts, (dc, ch 1, dc) in next st, dc in last st. Fasten off. Turn.

Row 4: Attach C with a sc in first st, sc in next st, work same as Row 2 beginning at *. Fasten off.

Row 5: With D, work same as Row 3. Fasten off. Turn.

When Row 1 of the scarf is complete, it will consist of a long fsc tail on each side of the hood, and a row of sc across the bottom edge of the hood.

Row 6: Repeat Row 4. Fasten off. Turn.

Row 7: With B, work same as Row 3. Fasten off. Turn.

Row 8: Attach A with a sc in first st, sc in next st, work same as Row 2 beginning at *. Fasten off.

4 Hood and Scarf Edging, Including Buttonhole and Button Placket

With RS facing and larger hook, attach D with a sc in opposite (chain) side of scarf fsc at right hand edge, working towards hood, sc in each fsc to corner where hood meets scarf, sc in next dc row end (end of Row 1 of hood), ch 3, working in opposite (chain) side of hood front edge, skip first 2 sts, sc in next st (buttonhole made), sc in each st across hood. Turn.

Make Button Placket
Row 1 (WS): Ch 1, sc in each of next 3 sts; leave remaining sts of hood front edge unworked. Turn.

Row 2: Sc in each of next 2 sts, 3 sc in next st for corner; working down side edge of button placket, sc in next sc row end; 2 sc in next dc row end (end of Row 1 of hood). Sc3tog evenly over inside corner where hood meets scarf.

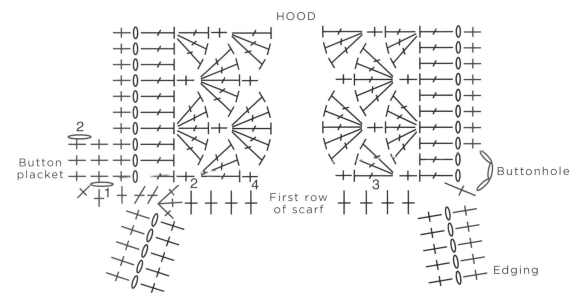

HOOD

Button placket

Buttonhole

First row of scarf

Edging

A stitch diagram and a close-up photo of the button placket.

QUICK REFERENCE

Sc3tog—The normal decrease for sc is done by working 2 stitches together. When 3 stitches are worked together in the same manner, it creates a 2-stitch decrease, appropriate for the inside edge of corners. Directions: (Insert hook in next st, yo and draw up a loop) 3 times. Yo and pull through all 4 loops on hook.

(continued)

Sc in opposite (chain) side of each fsc across scarf left side, 3 sc in corner, sc evenly spaced across end of scarf, 3 sc in next corner, sc in each st and in each ch-1 sp across bottom (scalloped) edge of scarf, 3 sc in corner, sc evenly spaced across last short end of scarf, sl st to join to first st of edging. Fasten off.

5 Make Button

With H (5 mm) hook and D, follow the instructions for a button (page 172). Use the two yarn tails of the button, threaded on the yarn needle, to sew the button to the center of the button placket made as part of the edging in Step 4.

6 Hood Tassel

To make the single large tassel for the point of the hood, use all four colors, A, B, C, and D.

TIP Don't wrap too tightly. The strands of yarn should be snug, but not tightly stretched. If one or more colors run out, don't worry, the number of strands needed is approximate.

Holding one strand of each yarn, all four together, wrap around the piece of cardboard, or the short-side direction around a DVD movie case. Wrap 10 times, for a total of 40 strands wrapped. Cut all four strands from any leftover yarn.

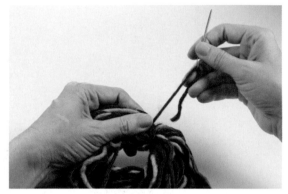

Thread yarn needle with 36" (91.5 cm) length of color D. Slide all loops off the cardboard or DVD case and run the yarn needle through the center of the loops, about 12" (30.5 cm). Bring the needle over the top (outside) of the loops and pass through again. Repeat one more time, to begin the binding at the tassel's top.

Pull both ends firmly to tighten. Tie short and long ends together firmly at the top of the binding stitch just created. Remove needle and re-thread it onto the long end of the binding yarn.

Hold the bound bundle of loops so that about an inch sticks out of your fist. Wrap the long end of the binding yarn around the bundle of loops, five times firmly.

Pass the needle under the wraps, through the top binding, back up to the top binding knot. Remove needle.

Turn the tassel around and insert scissors through all loops. Pull taut and cut straight across. After the cut is made, bunch all the strands together again, and trim any strands that somehow ended up longer than the rest, so all strands have uniform length.

Use the smaller crochet hook to pull the two ends of the tassel's binding strand through the tip of the hood. Tie securely to the yarn tail left there in step 2.

7 Scarf Tassels, Make Six

With D, repeat hood tassel instructions, wrapping a single strand of yarn 12 times around the cardboard or DVD case.

8 Finishing

Weave in all yarn tails securely. Block gently by spritzing with cool water, finger shaping for flat corners, and allowing to dry flat.

Using binding strands, sew three tassels to each end of scarf. Sew one tassel to each corner and one to the center of each end.

Abbreviations and Symbols

Here is the list of standard abbreviations used for crochet.

approx	approximately	p	picot
beg	begin/beginning	patt	pattern
bet	between	pc	popcorn
BL	back loop(s)	pm	place marker
bo	bobble	prev	previous
BP	back post	qutr	quadruple triple crochet
BPdc	back post double crochet	rem	remain/remaining
BPsc	back post single crochet	rep	repeat(s)
BPtr	back post triple crochet	rev sc	reverse single crochet
CC	contrasting color	rnd(s)	round(s)
ch	chain	RS	right side(s)
ch-	refers to chain or space previously made, e.g., ch-1 space	sc	single crochet
		sc2tog	single crochet 2 stitches together
ch lp	chain loop	sk	skip
ch-sp	chain space	Sl st	slip stitch
CL	cluster(s)	sp(s)	space(s)
cm	centimeter(s)	st(s)	stitch(es)
cont	continue	tbl	through back loop(s)
dc	double crochet	tch	turning chain
dc2tog	double crochet 2 stitches together	tfl	through front loop(s)
dec	decrease/decreases/decreasing	tog	together
dtr	double treble	tr	triple crochet
FL	front loop(s)	trtr	triple treble crochet
foll	follow/follows/following	tr2tog	triple crochet 2 together
FP	front post	TS	Tunisian simple stitch
FPdc	front post double crochet	WS	wrong side(s)
FPsc	front post single crochet	yd	yard(s)
FPtr	front post triple crochet	yo	yarn over
g	gram(s)	yoh	yarn over hook
hdc	half double crochet	[ ]	Work instructions within brackets as many times as directed.
inc	increase/increases/increasing		
lp(s)	loop(s)	*	Repeat instructions following the single asterisk as directed.
Lsc	long single crochet		
m	meter(s)	* *	Repeat instructions between asterisks as many times as directed or repeat from a given set of instructions.
MC	main color		
mm	millimeter(s)		
oz	ounce(s)		

Term Conversions

Crochet techniques are the same universally, and everyone uses the same terms. However, US patterns and UK patterns are different because the terms denote different stitches. Here is a conversion chart to explain the differences.

US	UK
single crochet (sc)	double crochet (dc)
half double crochet (hdc)	half treble (htr)
double crochet (dc)	treble (tr)
triple crochet (tr)	double treble (dtr)

Stitch Key

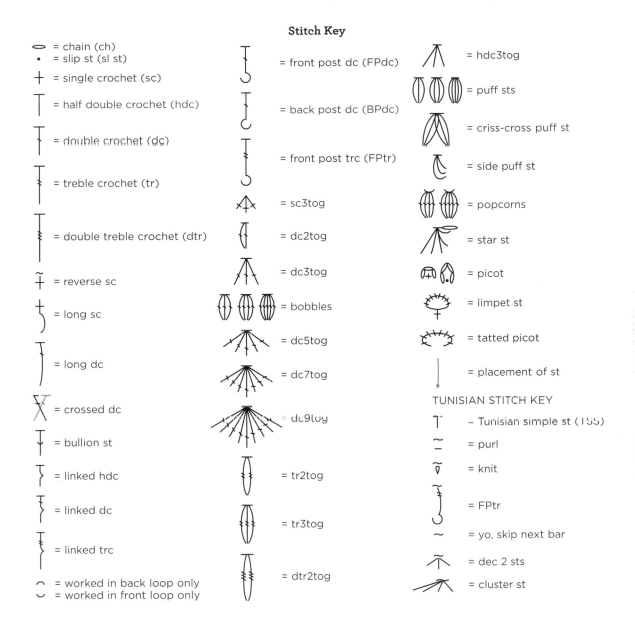

- ⬯ = chain (ch)
- • = slip st (sl st)
- + = single crochet (sc)
- ⊤ = half double crochet (hdc)
- ⊤ = double crochet (dc)
- ⊤ = treble crochet (tr)
- ⊤ = double treble crochet (dtr)
- ~⊤ = reverse sc
- long sc
- long dc
- ⤬ = crossed dc
- bullion st
- linked hdc
- linked dc
- linked trc
- ⌒ = worked in back loop only
- ⌣ = worked in front loop only

- = front post dc (FPdc)
- = back post dc (BPdc)
- = front post trc (FPtr)
- = sc3tog
- = dc2tog
- = dc3tog
- = bobbles
- = dc5tog
- = dc7tog
- = dc9tog
- = tr2tog
- = tr3tog
- = dtr2tog

- = hdc3tog
- = puff sts
- = criss-cross puff st
- = side puff st
- = popcorns
- = star st
- = picot
- = limpet st
- = tatted picot
- = placement of st

TUNISIAN STITCH KEY

- = Tunisian simple st (TSS)
- ~ = purl
- = knit
- = FPtr
- ~ = yo, skip next bar
- = dec 2 sts
- = cluster st

Glossary

Drape. The ability of a fabric to interact with gravity. Stiff fabrics hold their shape, resisting gravity's pull and do NOT drape. Fabric with a high degree of drape will fold gently without stiff creases. It will hang in soft folds when held by a corner. Good drape is a goal in making garments. However, in sculptural, three-dimensional objects, drape might be a drawback.

Felting (felted). A process using heat, moisture, and friction, in which wool fibers are forced to meld together. Felting makes a fabric solid, dense, and nearly waterproof. When an item is felted, it usually shrinks by about 30% of its original size. Only hair from a sheep or goat will felt, so choose yarns with 75% or more wool and/or mohair content for felting. 100% is best. Some dyes affect a yarn's ability to felt; so even within the same brand of wool yarn, some colors may felt more densely than others. "Superwash" or washable wools have been treated to prevent shrinkage, which means they also will not felt.

Gauge. The number of stitches in each horizontal inch of row, and the number of rows in each vertical inch. Gauge is usually measured over 4" of a 6 × 6" swatch. This prevents the first and last row, and first and last stitch from being counted. Those commonly are NOT the same size as the rest of the work, and gauge is meant to measure the size and shape of the average stitch in the fabric. Gauge is usually stated at the beginning of a pattern. If the finished object is to be the same size as the designer's, then the stitches must each be the same size. Use the hook that will create correct gauge, not necessarily the same hook as that used by the designer.

Picot. "Little point"—a picot is any small point or loop sticking out from a smooth edge, made intentionally for decorative purposes. Tension. The tightness or looseness with which yarn is held and moved while crocheting. Some older patterns and patterns in UK terms use the words "tension" and "gauge" interchangeably.

Stitch definition. The ability of a fabric to show distinct stitch details in its surface. If the colors are busy, or the yarn is fuzzy, the individual shapes of fancy stitches do not show. Generally, if the stitch pattern is fancy, then it's a good idea to choose a plain, smooth yarn to enhance stitch definition. On the other hand, if the yarn is fancy in its color/texture, then choose simple stitch patterns, knowing that stitch definition will be compromised by the yarn.

Superwash. A treatment given to wool yarns to make them resist the felting process. Superwash wools can be washed in warm water. The process also often results in extra softness, making superwash wools great choices for children's items—where there's a need for both softness and washability.

Swatch(es). Small pieces made before starting a project. Swatches are used to measure gauge, determine a yarn's response to blocking or washing, determine how much a fabric will stretch out, determine color pooling issues, and to practice new skills or stitch patterns. Making swatches is the best way to determine the correct hook size to use for a project.

Tail, yarn tail. The strand of yarn that is left from the beginning of a piece's foundation. It should always be at least 4-6" long, for weaving in securely. Some patterns will direct that a longer tail be left when starting. In this case it's usually because the tail will be used in seaming.

Tension. The tightness or looseness with which yarn is held and moved while crocheting. Some older patterns and patterns in UK terms use the words "tension" and "gauge" interchangeably.

Working yarn. The strand of yarn that runs from the yarn ball to the work. This is the yarn that is moved and incorporated into each new stitch. In crochet, it is generally held to the back of the work, away from the crocheter, and the hook passes through the work to interact with the working yarn.

About the Author

Deb Burger learned to crochet from her grandmother at age 12. While she has found enjoyment in many artforms, crochet remains her lifelong favorite. She has been teaching crochet for the past 20 years through Girl Scouting, various community centers, summer camps, at Charlotte's Fibers (a yarn shop in Western North Carolina), and the John C. Campbell Folk School. She is active in the online community, Ravelry as Cerdeb, and has written articles and patterns for Interweave Crochet and the e-zines *Crochet Insider* and *Crochet Uncut*. Deb and her musician/potter husband Don live in a small town in the mountains of East Tennessee. They are the parents of 7 grown children and grandparents of 4, most of whom also crochet. In addition to crochet, Deb enjoys knitting, embroidery, painting, fiber sculpture, gardening, performing folk music, and reading.

Index

DON'T MISS THE OTHER BOOKS IN THE SERIES!

Knitting 101
Carri Hammett
ISBN: 9781589236462

Sewing 101
ISBN: 9781589235748

Quilting 101
ISBN: 9781589235731

Beading 101
Karen Mitchell
and Ann Mitchell
ISBN: 9781589236653

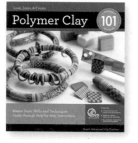

Polymer Clay 101
Angela Mabray
and Kim Otterbein
ISBN: 9781589234703

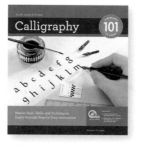

Calligraphy 101
Jeaneen Gauthier
ISBN: 9781589235038

Origami 101
Benjamin John Coleman
ISBN: 9781589236066

MORE BOOKS ON CROCHETING

**The Complete Photo
Guide to Crochet**
Margaret Hubert
ISBN: 9781589234727

Plus Size Crochet
Margaret Hubert
ISBN: 9781589233393

The Granny Square Book
Margaret Hubert
ISBN: 9781589236387

**AVAILABLE ONLINE OR AT
YOUR LOCAL CRAFT OR BOOK STORE.**

Creative Publishing
international

www.CreativePub.com

OUR BOOKS ARE AVAILABLE AS E-BOOKS, TOO!

Many of our bestselling titles are now available as E-Books.
Visit www.Qbookshop.com to find links to e-vendors!